GW00401781

C.S. LEWIS
AND THE ISLAND
OF HIS BIRTH

C.S. LEWIS
AND THE ISLAND
OF HIS BIRTH

THE PLACES, THE STORIES, THE INSPIRATION

BY

SANDY SMITH

lagan
press

lagan press

Published by

Lagan Press

All correspondence to

Lagan Press

Verbal Arts Centre

Stable Lane & Mall Wall

Bishop Street Within

Derry-Londonderry

BT48 6PU

ISBN: 978 1 908188 44 1 (hbk)

978 1 908188 45 8 (pbk)

Author: Sandy Smith

Title: C.S. Lewis and the Island of his Birth

First published: 2013

Printed by W&G Baird Ltd, Caulside Drive, Antrim BT41 2RS

Tourism Ireland, Beresford House, 2 Beresford Road,
Coleraine, Northern Ireland, BT52 1GE, Telephone 02870 359200

The Ulster-Scots Agency, 68-72 Great Victoria Street,
Belfast, Northern Ireland, BT2 7BB. Telephone: 028 9023 1113

To my wife Norma

and our grandchildren

Ethan and Jacob.

In the hope that Ethan and Jacob come to embrace the thinking of all true Narnians.

CONTENTS

PREFACE

Circular Road is not exactly a misnomer for the road in East Belfast where C.S. Lewis spent his boyhood. As an adjective for the approximate shape of the road, it is accurate enough in that the road is roughly semi-circular in shape when viewed in plan. It leaves the Holywood Road to the right at the junction with Station Road as one travels out from the City in the direction of Holywood and sweeps in a semi-circular arc, rejoining the main Holywood Road almost a mile further on.

It was when Norma and I went to live on the Circular Road in 1979, five years after we were married, that our interest in C.S. Lewis's connections with Belfast began to grow. Previously, during the years of my own undergraduate studies at Queen's University in Belfast, I had read some books written by Lewis that intrigued me and captured my imagination. My introduction to Lewis had been through books such as *The Problem of Pain*,

Junction of Holywood Road and Circular Road

Miracles and *Surprised by Joy*. His apologetics were particularly meaningful to me at a stage in life when I was first encountering the struggle with life's big questions. Initially, it was not simply that I felt Lewis had answered the questions surrounding the existence of pain, suffering and evil in our world that was of greatest appeal to me. On reflection, I am not even sure that on a first reading I understood fully the strengths and weaknesses of his arguments. The appeal for me lay in the fact that someone considered these questions to be not

Holywood Rd with St Mark's Church in the distance

intractable. I was interested by the notion advanced by Lewis, that the existence of pain, suffering and evil in our world could not be used with complete, authoritative and unanswerable certainty as an argument to promote the idea that our universe is the inevitable product of mindless evolutionary processes. That Lewis was prepared to appeal to reason and to offer a reasoned argument that dealt with the big questions but retained a belief in the God of historic Christianity I found more than interesting. I feel indebted to Lewis for his contributions on the big questions and to his ability to make the debate appealing,

understandable and interesting to people from a wide range of backgrounds. Chad Walsh (1914 – 1991 Professor of English at Beloit College, Wisconsin) styled Lewis as "Apostle to the Sceptics" in his book of the same title. For me, Lewis is well deserving of this designation. My own instinctive tendency towards scepticism has been appropriately checked and balanced by Lewis's lucid lines of argument and I owe to him a debt of gratitude for the fact

Circular Road where it rejoins the Holywood Road

that my own focus and belief remain embedded in historic Christianity.
It is this sense of indebtedness that is partly responsible for this book.

By the time our own children were old enough to read or be read to, we
were living on Circular Road in East Belfast and just a few houses away
from Little Lea, the boyhood home of C.S. Lewis. When the children
were young, we would often go for walks through Cairnburn Park.
On these walks we usually passed Little Lea on our way home and in
winter days when the leaves were off the trees the house could be seen
very clearly. Sometimes, in the
dusky dark of a winter afternoon,
the children would point to the
house and ask, "Is that the house
where the wardrobe was?" In truth,
at that particular time, although we
had read *The Lion, the Witch and the
Wardrobe* we were unaware of the
actual story of the real wardrobe. It
was not until later that we became
aware of many of the facts about
C.S. Lewis's life and the genesis of
some of his stories but there was a
real wardrobe with its own particular

Little Lea - the Belfast house where C.S. Lewis spent his boyhood years

significance in the Lewis story and that has its roots in East Belfast.

The beginnings of our more detailed awareness were probably crystallised
by a project that was undertaken by our daughter Cherith during her P6
year at Strandtown Primary School.   She arrived home from school one
day asking if we could suggest anything of local interest that she might
make into a project as part of her work at school. We suggested a project
on C.S. Lewis and his links with that part of Belfast immediately around
where we lived. We took some photos, made a call to the rector of the
local Church of Ireland congregation, assisted Cherith to draw some maps
and soon the bones of an interesting P6 project began to emerge. From
there my own personal interest snowballed. Norma and I have read
extensively on Lewis and we began to re-read many of the books that we
had enjoyed previously.

In 1998, a centenary conference was arranged at Queen's University in Belfast to mark one hundred years from Lewis's birth in the city. It was here that we first met up with many other local Lewis enthusiasts including David Bleakley who published *C.S. Lewis at Home in Ireland* and Ross Wilson who completed 'The Searcher' sculpture to mark the centenary year. After the centenary year a group was formed to promote a local C.S. Lewis Association in Belfast. I was a founder member of that group along with Alistair Coey, Michael Wardlow and others. Although the group eventually ceased to meet regularly, one of the outcomes of that venture was the establishing of a C.S. Lewis Tour in Belfast and I began conducting the tour under the auspices of Belfast City Council. The tour is currently a popular three-hour lecture tour that takes in the most significant locations in Belfast associated with C.S. Lewis, his writing and his family.

The tour has prompted requests for information along with requests for lectures and talks to a diverse range of interested groups. These talks formed the basis of a series of lectures, parts of which have been delivered to audiences in a variety of places but including the Linen Hall

The Marion E Wade Centre in Wheaton, Illinois

Library in Belfast, the Milwaukee Irish Festival in Wisconsin, Wheaton College in Illinois, and at the Oklahoma Baptist University in Shawnee, USA. It is intended to repeat the series of lectures on a regular basis as a short course at Belmont Tower in Belfast which now houses the C.S. Lewis Centre of which I am currently the Director.

It was first suggested to me by Marjorie Lamp-Meade at Wheaton that I should give some consideration to doing something with the Lewis material I had put together and to preserve it for future generations. Following some lectures I gave to mark the commencement of the C.S. Lewis Centre at Belmont Tower in Belfast, Alf McCreary, the religion correspondent for the *Belfast Telegraph,* also suggested that the material should be put together into some kind of permanent record. These, among suggestions from others, including the former director of the Linen Hall Library in Belfast, Brian Adgey, pointed up to me the fact that in Northern Ireland we have been slow to promote our unique links to a Belfast author of international reputation. While Lewis has an international audience through his books that are now translated into forty-two languages it continues to surprise and delight me when people join my tour and announce excitedly that they were previously unaware that he was born in Belfast. It is likely that other centres around the world will celebrate Lewis's work more fully and with a larger budget than the current centre in Belfast but none can replicate our unique link with Lewis and his family. It is not possible to stand at Lewis's birthplace without coming to Belfast, Northern Ireland.

A number of books have been written about Lewis's life. Many more have been written about his work. Films have been made about his books and about his marriage to Joy Gresham (née Davidman). This book is aimed specifically at celebrating his Irish roots and updating his readers on the locations in which he spent his boyhood. It is in Belfast that the genesis of many of his books is to be found. It was here that he and his immediate ancestors called home. This book is about C.S. Lewis and the island of his birth.

I want to acknowledge not only those who sparked the idea for this book but those who provided invaluable assistance in translating it into a reality. Notably my wife Norma whose help and support ensured the completion of this project. Norma has shared my interest in Lewis over the years and together we have spent many hours in pleasurable conversation discussing his views, the details of his life and his links to Belfast. Her specific input to this publication has been as an enthusiastic and diligent editor and her work has contributed to the accuracy of this book. I also want to acknowledge the significant contribution of Tourism Ireland (TI) and the Ulster-Scots Agency (The Agency) for their interest from the outset. The personal support from Jim Millar (The Agency) and Aubrey Irwin (TI) has smoothed the path to publication.

Circular Road, Belfast, at Little Lea

As we approach the memorial of fifty years since the death of this significant Belfast author, it is important to record the images from around the island of his birth and the associated narrative that links Lewis and his family to Belfast, to the north coast of Northern Ireland, to the Kingdom of Mourne, to Dublin and to Cork. With the passing of time, many of the landmarks so familiar to Lewis and his family are in danger of falling foul of the developers. One of the positive side effects of the current and otherwise unwanted economic recession is that for the time being at least, the bulldozers are moving slowly and significant elements of the Irish landscape, north and south, remain as they were in the years when the Lewis family lived in Belfast.

This book is presented as a record of the places that shaped the early development of the creator of Narnia. Lewis's success was not only in creating the characters and landscapes of Narnia but also in his description of the issues that posed a threat to Narnia and how these threats were dealt with. The issues underlying the threats to his imagined world are real enough and still evident to some extent in the island of his birth and throughout our increasingly unstable world.

It is my hope and intention that the images and information presented in this book will benefit not only tourists who come to visit Ireland, north and south, but a new generation of Lewis scholars, students, casual readers and children who will enjoy the literary legacy he has left to us.

Sandy Smith
Belfast, Northern Ireland
1 January 2013

Doorknob at St Mark's Rectory

Chapter One

BEGINNINGS IN BELFAST

INTRODUCTION

C.S. Lewis was born in Belfast in 1898. This is still a source of surprise to some visitors to the City and indeed to some permanent residents. Many avid readers of Lewis's work admit that they had never consciously noted that he was Irish by birth. Local Lewis enthusiasts respond to such admissions sometimes with amazement tinged with a sense of disappointment and sometimes with amazement tinged with pleasure. The pleasure stems from the opportunity that is created to surprise and interest our visitors

Narnia benches at Holywood Arches, Belfast

with the additional information about Lewis's life and work and thereby add to their knowledge of the cultural and literary history of Belfast while the slight sense of disappointment arises from the fact that in Belfast, we have been all too slow to publicise our links to Lewis. Regardless of the accuracy of his readers' knowledge or their perceptions, two facts remain: one, that to many, he was and always will be, famous as the Oxford don who has left for us a rich literary heritage, and number two, that he was born in Belfast on 29 November 1898.

Previous photo: Belfast City Hall

The City of Belfast

Belfast is a name of ancient Gaelic origin but there is some ambiguity as to its precise meaning. There is a suggestion that the name refers to a sandbank that hundreds of years ago enabled travellers to cross the river Lagan on which Belfast is built. At low tide, the river could be crossed at the sandbank which was located close to the present site of the Queen's Bridge and near where the River Farset joins the widening estuary of the Lagan.

Although Belfast celebrates the four hundreth anniversary of its founding charter in 2013, its history goes back much further to settlements that preceded the excursions of the Normans to these islands. Today, however, there are few remnants of those early beginnings and no physical trace remains even of the castle constructed at Belfast in the twelfth century, by the Normans who invaded eastern Ulster in that period. The only reminders of this ancient castle are in some of the street names such as Castle Street and Castle Lane and the large shopping centre CastleCourt which stands close to the site on which the castle was built. With the demise of Norman control in the fourteenth century, the area came within the influence of the Gaelic chieftains until the proposal by Queen Elizabeth I to establish an English settlement at Belfast. This proposal made little significant progress until the reign of James I. James became King of England and of Scotland at the Union of the Crowns in 1603 (see Chapter 2) and settlers of Scottish and English origin became involved in developing the region. James granted the castle at Belfast and the surrounding lands to Sir Arthur Chichester and in 1613 the Borough of Belfast was established by Royal Charter. The old Norman castle was destroyed by fire in 1708 and Lord Donegall built a new castle on the slopes of the Cave Hill in 1870. The Charter gave to the Chichester family the very considerable authority on which the City was built and the four hundred years of history since the granting of the Royal Charter establishing the City are etched on the streets of Belfast that bear names such as Chichester, May and Shaftesbury.

The Chichester family was granted extensive lands stretching from Belfast, through County Antrim to County Donegal (spelled with

Previous photo: View of the Queen's Bridge, Belfast

just one L) in the north-west. The family inherited the Donegall (spelled with two Ls) title but Lord Donegall declined to live in Ireland and it was the second Marquis of Donegall, George Augustus, who became the first of the Chichester family to live in Belfast. Eventually the Donegall lands and titles passed into the hands of the Shaftesburys but neither family played a major role in developing the industrial City of Belfast that was to emerge in the nineteenth century. The ninth Earl of Shaftesbury, grandson of Lord Donegall, inherited Belfast Castle. He became Mayor of the City in 1907 and the first Chancellor of Queen's University Belfast on its elevation from College to University in 1908. Shaftesbury presented Belfast Castle to the City in 1934 and today it is still owned and managed by Belfast City Council.

The Belfast into which C.S. Lewis was born in 1898 was very different to the Belfast of 2013 which commemorates the fiftieth memorial of his passing and four hundred years since the granting of its charter.

By the end of the nineteenth century Belfast was a city in a very rapid transition. During the first half of the nineteenth century, the population had grown numerically from some 20,000 at the end of the eighteenth century to a population of 100,000. Not only was the City experiencing a five-fold expansion numerically but the character of Belfast was changing from a commercial hub to an industrial city. The merchants and professional gentlemen who influenced affairs in the 1800s were giving way to the captains of industry who would provide the more significant influence during the 1900s. This shift is important in the Lewis story. The City into which he was born was the fastest growing port in the British Isles. Its economic growth and development during the period when Belfast was home to the Lewis family was driven largely by the twin pillars of shipbuilding and the manufacture of linen. These industries are both significant in the story of the Lewis family. The City in which C.S. Lewis was born had held at different times, the nickname of 'Linenopolis' or was alternatively referred to as the 'Athens of the North', each being used to emphasise either its industrial or cultural development. At the end of the eighteenth century, Belfast had

Sir Edward Harland: founding partner of Harland & Wolff

The Linen Hall in Belfast formerly on the site of the City Hall

built, with great civic pride, The Linen Hall which was completed in 1783 on a prestigious site on what was then the outskirts of the City. The building of the Linen Hall marked a zenith in the economic importance of the linen industry in Belfast. Important companies such as William Ewart and Son were extending their mills and adding powerloom factories to their plant. Already, however, the production of cotton had entered the scene and had it not been for the American Civil War, cotton might well have eclipsed the importance of Irish linen as an international commodity much earlier than it did. The linen barons in Belfast were experiencing difficult times around the time of Lewis's birth. Firms such as Malcolmson and Co and John Hind and Co had collapsed, while others were teetering on the brink of closure. However, the outbreak of World War I in 1914 rekindled the fortunes of an otherwise fading linen industry which continued during the war years. The years immediately after the war, however, marked the beginning of its steady decline.

Shipbuilding, on the other hand, was still on an upward trend. A number of small shipbuilding concerns had grown dramatically and a series of mergers would establish Belfast as the fastest-growing port in the British Isles. The City was set to become a world leader in shipbuilding. In 1858 a small iron shipbuilding yard was set up by Robert

Inscription on the Harland monument   Following photo: Samson and Goliath, the cranes of Harland & Wolff

Hickson of Eliza Street in Belfast, at the Queens Island, a seventeen-acre island created artificially by the spoil from the dredging operation to deepen the shipping channel to Belfast's Donegall Quay. Hickson's manager was then the young Edward Harland whose personal assistant was Gustav Wolff and in 1861 the firm merged with other small but growing firms to become known

as Harland & Wolff. From the middle of the century, Belfast was larger than Dublin and had more steam-powered ships using the port than Dublin and Cork combined. It was almost certainly this growth that persuaded two young entrepreneurs to establish another iron shipbuilding works in Belfast. The shipbuilding firm of MacIlwaine, Lewis and McCall is an important feature in the Lewis story which will be highlighted in Chapter 2. Workman and Clarke, MacIlwaine and McCall together rivalled, and at times surpassed, the output of Harland & Wolff with whom they also eventually merged. They contributed to the rapid expansion of shipbuilding in Belfast from 20,000 gross tons in 1881 to over 80,000 tons by the end of the decade in which C.S. Lewis was born. By the first decade of the twentieth century all the

smaller yards had merged and traded under the name of Harland & Wolff. Belfast had truly become a 'Titanic' port, the largest port in Ireland and a world leader as a centre for the building of ships. This was the City that shaped the early life of C.S. Lewis.

The large cranes that still dominate the skyline of the City, once the largest cranes in Europe, no longer produce the tonnage of shipping they were designed for. While the bold, black initials H & W, are strikingly visible high up on the

William Ewart - Mayor of Belfast 1859 and father-in-law of Flora Lewis's cousin Mary

structure of both cranes and still remind citizens and visitors in Belfast of Harland & Wolff and the City's maritime history, they could equally stand for **H**ello and **W**elcome and serve as a reminder that tourism has now replaced shipbuilding as one of the City's current economic drivers. The City welcomes its visitors and tourists. They are welcome to share in the maritime and industrial history that has shaped the present. They are also welcome to share in the City's literary heritage. Belfast's past has shaped the present, it shaped the people who were born and grew up in the city and many of these people are now helping still to shape not only the present but the future. C.S. Lewis was one of these people. Fifty years after his death, his books still sell by their millions. The Hollywood film industry has experienced a renewed interest in his life and work which will continue to be a significant focus of both stage and screen for the best part of the next decade at least, to complete what has been commenced during the best part of the last decade. The links between Lewis, his family and the city of his birth, indeed the island of his birth, are the subject of this book. In the remainder of this chapter, the locations in Belfast that are significant in his story are detailed.

The *Titanic* Memorial in Belfast

Dundela

C.S. Lewis was born in Dundela, an area in Belfast located immediately beside Strandtown. In 1898 both were little more than small villages on the outskirts of Belfast with green fields between them and the city centre. Two years before Lewis was born, the city boundaries were extended to include the fashionable suburbs of Strandtown, Belmont and Ballyhackamore to the east and Malone

Strandtown from Dundela Avenue

to the south. Today these suburbs are part of the urban sprawl that has seen the city spread and expand to fill the lower reaches of the Lagan Valley that cradled its birth. Strandtown and Dundela are in the east of the city and encompassed by the area that is normally referred to today simply as East Belfast.

In his book *Surprised by Joy* (SBJ) published by J.M. Dent and Co in 1955, Lewis metaphorically retraces his steps to his birthplace. He opens the book with the words:

"I was born in the winter of 1898 at Belfast, the son of a solicitor and of a clergyman's daughter" (1).

The sentence is interesting from a number of perspectives. It pinpoints the city of his birth and the year. It is interesting not only for its construction but for what it conveys of the times and perhaps of how he reflects on the

Oil painting of Dundela Villas - Alan Seaton

place, the period and the parents that were the occasion of his birth. While some of the details of the latter will be highlighted in Chapter 2, some of the other elements of the sentence will be left for consideration elsewhere but the subject of his book that is introduced by this sentence is of relevance here. The subtitle of *SBJ* is 'the shape of my early life'. His early life was shaped in Belfast. More importantly, the experience he recalls in the opening movements of *SBJ* is of major significance in his story. This experience of what he was ultimately to describe as 'JOY' occurred at the house in Dundela Avenue, Belfast where he was born.

The house was one of two in Dundela Avenue, that together were known as Dundela Villas. In the return for the 1901 Census of Ireland, the details entered for the house indicate that it was:

Dundela apartments now built on the location of Lewis's birthplace 'a second class dwelling, with 6 persons living in the house, occupying 7 rooms, and having five front windows'.

The six persons included the Lewis family and two servants whose names are recorded as Martha Barber, the children's nurse and Sarah Ann Conlon, the cook. According to the 1901 census, Martha was from County Monaghan but by the time Lewis's childhood memory was active she had married and moved on. Her marriage to Mr Thomas McBratney, then living at Athlone, left her post vacant and it was ultimately filled by Lizzie Endicott from County Down. It is Lizzie who is remembered by Lewis and it is to her that he attributes his sense of humour.

Plaque on apartments in Dundela Avenue

The view from the front windows of the house in Dundela Avenue was of the Antrim hills to the north and west of Belfast. These comprise the low peaks of Colin, Divis Mountain and the Cave Hill which is striking not only because of the caves in the steeply sloping hillside but because of the profile of its top and the castle constructed about halfway up. The profile of the Cave Hill, particularly as seen from such vantage points as Waring Street in the centre of the city, creates an impression of the face of a sleeping giant. Jonathan Swift who lived in the city and had a romantic attachment with the daughter of William Waring for whom Waring Street is named, is said to have been inspired by the profile of the Cave Hill to write *Gulliver's Travels* with its graphic image of the sleeping giant of Lilliput. Lewis, commenting on his favourite childhood books, says in the first chapter of *Surprised by Joy*, that E. Nesbit's children's trilogy was among his favourites, especially the last one, *The Amulet* but he records:

Profile of Cave Hill from Dundela Avenue

"Gulliver ... was one of my favourites" (2).

He owned an unabridged edition of *Gulliver's Travels* which had lots of illustrations and without doubt, one of the giant, lying horizontally as profiled in the view from his front window. The view from the front windows of the house in which Lewis was born not only had the profile of a sleeping giant but also nestling clearly on the slopes of the Cave Hill is Belfast Castle. The castle was designed by Lanyon and Lynn, a famous firm of local architects, who also

designed the Custom House and the University. The Castle was completed in 1870 for Lord Donegall, the third Marquis who was the first of the Chichester family to live in Belfast. Lewis's early life commenced with a view to the north of his home of a castle and a sleeping giant. In a famous quote recorded by his brother he indicates that it was the landscapes of the northern counties of Ireland that evoked mythical images, some of which came to populate the Narnian landscape half a century later.

Belfast Castle from Dundela

Lewis also records the impact that the view to the south, as seen from the nursery windows of Dundela Villas where he was born, had on him. In a very detailed passage in *Surprised by Joy*, where he records his first encounter with beauty, he comments on the 'Green Hills' to the south. These were his first glimpses of County Down. The low line of the Castlereagh Hills, although, in fact, not very far away in terms of distance, seemed to Lewis and his brother to be totally unattainable. His sense as a child was that he could see these hills but could not reach them. He tells us that it was the sight of these hills that created within him his first sense of longing, or an emotion better described by the German word *Sehnsucht*. As a child he would not have been aware of the historical significance of Castlereagh, its hills, the famous previous owner of the castle there and of the link with his own ancestors, the Hamiltons. Had he known the history, perhaps his sense of longing would have been more intense. This history of the Hamilton, the O'Neill and the Montgomery families will be outlined in Chapter 2.

The Garden at Dundela

The episodes that Lewis recalls from his childhood memories of growing up in Dundela Villas are not just of the sense of longing brought to him from looking through the nursery windows to the distant Castlereagh Hills but also his awareness of nature and the memory of how that awareness was awakened.

He records the story of how one morning his brother Warren, who was three years older than him, had been outside playing in the garden of their home where they both played almost every day. On this particular morning, Warnie,

as he was affectionately known, had been given the lid of a biscuit tin which
he took out into the garden. He gathered some moss from the garden and laid
it out on the lid of the biscuit tin to make it resemble a small lawn and he then
proceeded to place around it some flowers, some leaves , some twigs and a piece
of a flowering currant. When his piece of artwork was finished, Warnie brought
it inside the house to show to his younger brother.
Lewis recalls in great detail the impression it
made on him.   He remembers vividly its aesthetic
appearance. He remembers the smell of the
damp moss and of the flowering currant and he
remembers how he felt. His sense of longing was
aroused. On another morning a few years later
in another garden in Belfast he walked past a
flowering currant and the smell reminded him of
the toy garden created by his brother at Dundela.
He records his difficulty in finding suitable words

The garden at Dundela

to describe accurately the feelings he experienced. His feelings included a sense
of tension, of longing, of anxiety and of desire, something akin to Milton's
enormous bliss of Eden. It was, he says, undoubtedly desire but his question
was, "desire for what?" These were idyllic years in young Lewis's life.   There
was no cause for longing or anxiety, he was in good health, his parents were
well, they were affluent by the standard of the time, he enjoyed the company
and companionship of his brother and he lived in a large beautiful house with
a large and beautiful garden. Years later, he continued to ponder on where
this feeling had come from and how it had arisen. What was the source of his
longing or the object of his unfulfilled desire? He came to refer to this feeling
of unsatisfied desire, in a technical sense, as 'JOY'. This feeling of 'JOY' was
for him, different from feelings of either pleasure or happiness in a number
of respects but principally because it came like a stab, in moments when it
was unanticipated and unexpected. These were significant moments in his
life which he remembers in great detail and he goes on to say that the central
story of his life is about nothing else. This is an enormous claim to make for a
sensation that arose in a Belfast garden. Writing the concluding paragraph of
SBJ some fifty years later he claims that the old stab, the old bitter-sweet feeling
of longing, anxiety, *sehnsucht*, returned often over the course of his life. For him
its importance lay in the fact that it, the desire, pointed to something other and
something outer, something outside the experiences to be had in this world.
It is warmingly curious how he ends the book. The something outer and the

Following photo: Belfast Castle

something other he embodies in the notion of 'Jerusalem'. Not Jerusalem, the capital city of present-day Israel but of the Heavenly City. Lewis ends his book in a manner redolent of how St John concludes the Apocalypse with a reference to the city which contains its own hint of longing in the words "we would be at Jerusalem". This sense of longing was first experienced by Lewis in a garden in Belfast. It was a longing that could ultimately be satisfied only by an entrance to the Eternal City.

The theme of unsatisfied desire, prompted initially by his childhood experience in the garden of the house in Belfast where he was born, was built upon by Lewis many years later in his apologetics. It became an important philosophical concept, highlighted by others and described as the Argument from Desire. This sense of longing and the experience of joy were viewed by Lewis as arrows being shot at him since childhood. They begged a question as to their source. For many years he desperately did not want to accept that their source was 'other' or 'outer' in the sense of coming from beyond our world. He did not want to accept the possibility that there might be worlds other than our own, but finally, the author of *The Chronicles of Narnia* comes to a different conclusion. Long before he wrote *The Chronicles of Narnia*, he writes in *Mere Christianity*:

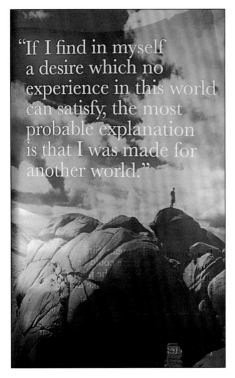

Quotation in C.S. Lewis reading room at QUB

"If I find in myself a desire which no experience in this world can satisfy, the most probable explanation is that I was made for another world." (3)

The quotation is featured on the walls of the C.S. Lewis reading room in the new McClay Library in Queen's University, Belfast. The room makes an interesting visit.

It is entered by going through a door fashioned in the style of a wardrobe door and its centrepiece is a large round table topped with glass which covers a circular map of Narnia. *The Chronicles of Narnia* are an exploration of another world filled with dreams, longings and desires that for Lewis commenced in a garden in Belfast.

C.S. Lewis reading room

St Mark's Church, Holywood Road, Belfast

St Mark's Parish Church

Dundela Villas where Lewis was born is in the parish of St Mark's, Dundela.
His grandfather, the Rev Thomas R. Hamilton, was the rector of St Mark's
from 1874 and baptised both of his grandsons in the font that stands just
inside the entrance to the church and beneath the tower which rises to 183
feet on the west wall of the building. Lewis was christened Clive Staples
Lewis on 29 January 1899. The Staples name came from his maternal
grandfather's side of the family. His great-grandfather, Hugh Hamilton,
married Elizabeth Staples and her maiden name was used in the names of
her children. So Staples became a family name which passed to C.S. The
name Clive probably has associations with India in the form of the Robert
Clive, formerly governor of Bengal and known as Clive of India.   Lewis's
grandfather had served as a chaplain in India and the Empire was still a
prominent feature of interest in the British Isles at the time of his grandson's
birth. Although he was christened Clive Staples, he styled himself as 'Jack'
when still little more than a toddler and it was as Jack that he was known
for virtually all of his life.

C.S. 'Jack' Lewis - Ulsterman

How he came to be called Jack is not known for certain. What is certain is that it was an early development insisted upon by Lewis himself. A few commentators have offered explanations that are not very convincing and in 1986 I undertook to write to a relation of Lewis's, a lady called Beth Tate (née Lewis) then living in Loughborough, Leicestershire. I say 'I' wrote but actually it was a family venture undertaken by my wife, Norma, as part of my daughter's P6 school project referred to in the preface. Beth informed us that the name arose following one of the Lewis family's regular summer holidays to the north coast. His mother, one of the

11.2.86

42, Main Street,
Sutton Bonacton
(near), Loughborough,
Leicestershire.

Dear Mrs Smith,

I hope that the enclosed letter will be of use to Cherith, good luck with the project! I am glad that the illuminated letter sent to my grandfather (who was C.S. Lewis' uncle) is in good hands in St. Marks. He was also a very remarkable man, but unfortunately he died at an early age.

With best wishes,
Yours sincerely, Beth Tate.

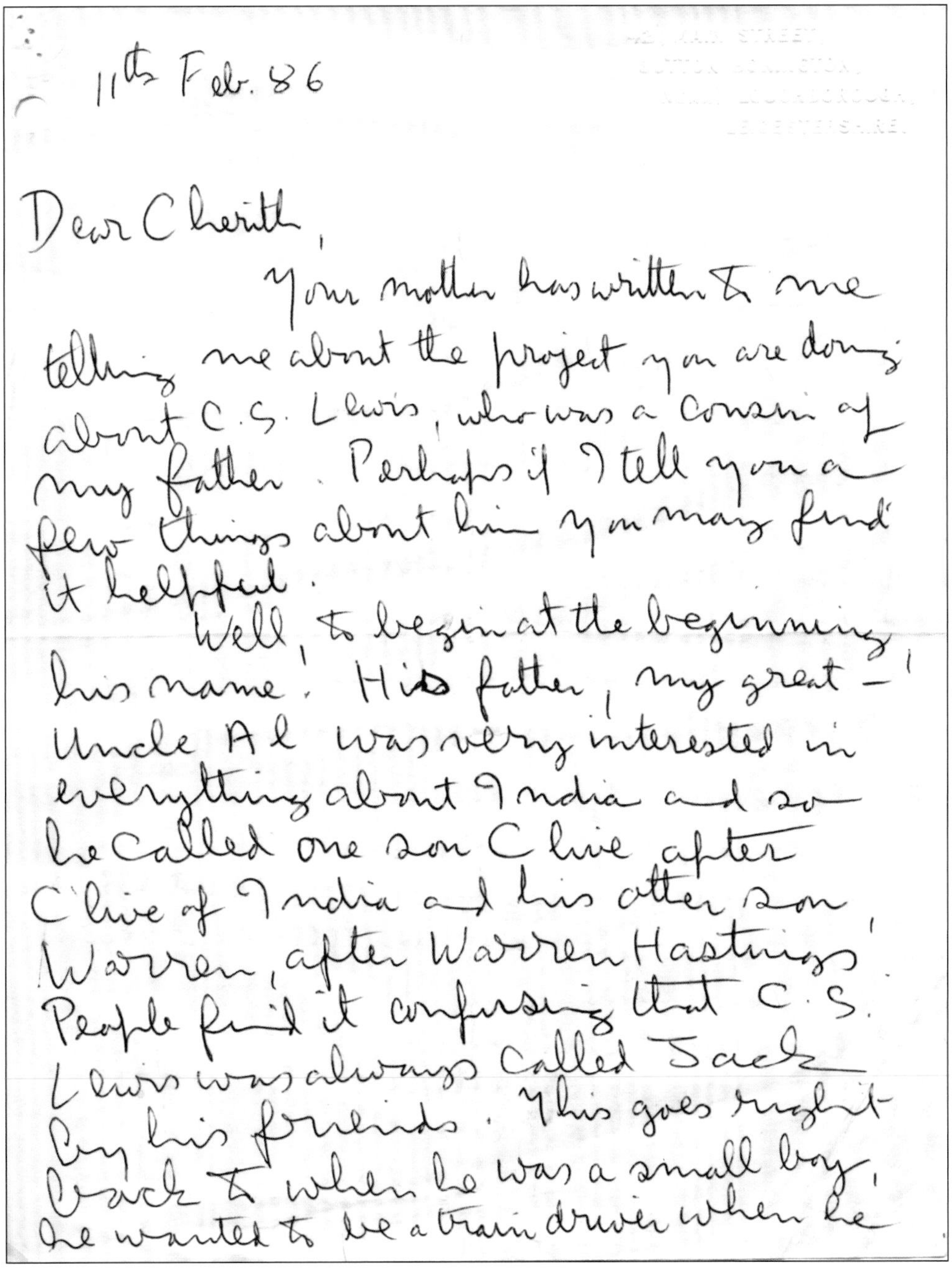

11th Feb. 86

Dear Cherith,

Your mother has written to me telling me about the project you are doing about C.S. Lewis, who was a cousin of my father. Perhaps if I tell you a few things about him you may find it helpful.

Well, to begin at the beginning, his name! His father, my great-Uncle Al was very interested in everything about India and so he called one son Clive after Clive of India and his other son Warren, after Warren Hastings! People find it confusing that C.S. Lewis was always called Jack by his friends. This goes right back to when he was a small boy, he wanted to be a train driver when he

servants and the two Lewis children would annually travel by train from Belfast to Castlerock in County Londonderry.

Somehow they got to know that one of the train drivers was called Jack. The Lewis boys both loved trains and loved travelling by train. On arrival at their destination in Castlerock, young Lewis, still learning to talk, proudly announced "me Jacksie" and from that summer holiday on, Jack he became and Jack he remained. Many of his letters are signed Jack or simply J and certainly the references to him in the letters and diaries of his brother and father regularly use the letter J as an understood designation.

Following photo: Beach at Castlerock

grew up and the only train driver he
knew was called Jack! So he got the nickname.

When I was young we went
to Newcastle each year for our summer
holidays and C.S. Lewis came and
stayed with his brother in Kilkeel.
We used to go and have tea with them
which was a bit alarming as they
were both batchelors and believed in
giving children very plain food. He
loved walking over the Mourne
mountains, he never owned a car,
always preferring to walk.

A very interesting book about C.S. Lewis
has been written for young people, perhaps
you have heard of it! It is called
"The Secret Country of C.S. Lewis" by
Anne Arnott, published by Lakeland
it is a paperback book and is nicely illustrated,
I think you would enjoy reading it. (although

the writer does'nt know about the train-driver!)

When I grew up and met him again in Offord, I wondered if he would have changed a lot, but he was just the same as he had been when we were young, still walking everywhere!

He spent a great deal of his time writing to people all over the world, answering their questions about their religious beliefs. Anne Arnot tells us, in her book, that just before he died he wrote to a little girl a letter which included these words: "If you continue to love Jesus, nothing much can go wrong with you, and I hope you may always do so." I am sure he would have said the same to you, if he had known you.

Yours sincerely, Beth (Lewis) Tate.

Font at St Mark's

The font in which the Lewis brothers were baptised still occupies its original position beneath the tall tower of St Mark's. Its location was specified by the church architect, William Butterfield, a famous architect of the time who interestingly also designed the Chapel at Keble College in Oxford. The significance of this point will be referred to in Chapter 3. It was Butterfield who included several features in the architecture of St Mark's that we find reflected in Jack's writing. One of the features of the church is the pattern of tiles immediately in front of the font on the floor of the tower. The pattern forms a series of chevrons that point along the nave of the church in the direction of the sanctuary at the east wall. The chevrons are pointing in a horizontal direction. Butterfield used this motif as a device to highlight the notion of direction just as he used the tower itself. The tower terminates at its top with a pointed roof and a spire pointing vertically upward while the chevrons in the floor point horizontally along the length of the church. The length of the church is 183 feet, the same length as the height of the tower. While the tower and spire point heavenward, the chevrons point to the cross, located on the east wall, but elevated above the other significant church furniture. Butterfield's idea in using both of these devices was to highlight the notion of a journey, or we could substitute two other significant words for the same idea. The idealised journey, commencing

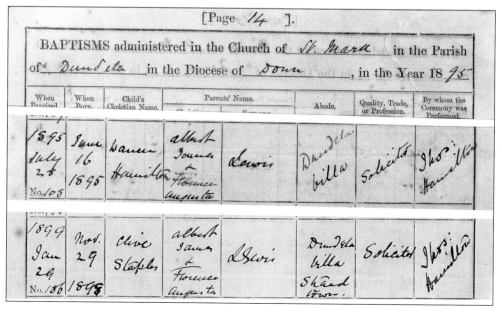

Baptismal entries for C.S. Lewis and his brother Warren

with an infant's baptism, Butterfield depicted as terminating in one dimension at the cross, a powerful Christian symbol of all that life ultimately means. The journey from the font to the final destination could be described using alternative words as life's pilgrimage or voyage. Both of these ideas are used significantly in two of the books Lewis wrote: *The Pilgrim's Regress* and *The Voyage of the Dawn Treader*. This same terminology, used in the context of a baptismal service for infants of the congregation in St Mark's, would have

The Baptisimal Register at St Mark's 1889 - 1904

impacted on Jack and through hearing it repeated from time to time in the baptismal service for other children the idea would have buried itself deep in his thinking. This leads to the question as to whether or not there is any evidence in his writing that these ideas of pilgrimage or of a particular destination or goal at the end of life's journey or voyage were shaped by his growing up in this congregation in Belfast. This question will be addressed in Chapter 4 in the section dealing with the window installed in the church by Jack and Warnie in memory of their parents.

The Lion

Jack's mother, Flora, as a girl in Belfast, was a daughter of the manse. St Mark's was built in Belfast in 1878 complete with its new manse provided for the Rector and his family. Flora spent her teenage years living there and right up until her marriage in 1894. The rectory was the home of Jack's grandparents and undoubtedly, even after his grandfather retired from his post, he stood at the front door of the rectory which is just adjacent to the church looking intently at the doorknob just above the letter box on the rectory door. On any other rectory door, the pattern of the door furniture might be merely an accidental or an incidental detail, but not on this rectory door. This is the rectory of St Mark's. The church icon for St Mark is the lion, and the Church was referred to locally as the Lion on the Hill (see J.C. Beckett – *The Lion on the Hill*) a reference to that part of the Holywood Road known as Bunkers Hill, the church magazine for this church is called *The Lion* and appropriately the

Door of the old rectory at St Mark's

brass knob on the rectory door is cast in the form of the head of a very severe-looking lion. Where did Jack encounter the first image of a lion that impressed him? The answer is that it was very likely the lion on the front doorknob of his grandfather's rectory and his mother's former home. In a letter to his publisher in response to a request for some information as to the origins of the images that bring the Narnian Chronicles to life, Jack indicates that many had been there from his teenage years or earlier. Many of these images were formed in his childhood. He says in *SBJ* that at the age of six, seven and eight:

"I was living almost entirely in my imagination or at least that the imaginative experience of those years now seems to me more important than anything else."(4)

Was the lion part of this imagery? Certainly yes; he tells us:

"I pored endlessly over an almost complete set of old 'Punches' which stood in my father's study. Tenniel gratified my passion for 'dressed animals' with his Russian bear, British LION, Egyptian crocodile and the rest." (5)

Did he know about the association of the lion with St Mark's? The evidence for this will be reviewed in Chapter 4.

Belfast's City Hall

In the previous paragraphs that provide a short introduction to, and a brief history of, the City of Belfast, reference was made to the linen industry and to the Linen Hall established in 1876 to promote the City's trade in linen. In the year that C.S. Lewis was born, the Linen Hall was demolished and the site cleared to make way for the building of the new City Hall in Belfast. The building of the City Hall was the happening event during Lewis's boyhood. The project commenced in 1898 and was completed in 1906, when Lewis was eight years old. The City Hall still occupies the site to the present day and is very much the centre of the City. Its relevance to the Lewis story is not

Donegall Square and City Hall, Belfast

just that it commenced in the year that he was born but also in that his father worked for the then Belfast City Corporation. As noted earlier, Jack's father, Albert Lewis, was a solicitor. He was in fact the prosecuting solicitor in the Belfast Police Courts of the time. The administration of the law courts and of the police service was under the control of the City Corporation in those days, an arrangement that no longer exists today and so the City Corporation was one of Albert Lewis's major clients. Details

Queen Victoria statue at Belfast City Hall

83 Royal Ave. Site of Albert Lewis's legal offices

of developments in the building of the City Hall would have featured around the dinner table when Albert returned to the family home of an evening. On the occasions of his visits to the city centre, Jack saw this building rise out of the ground and with it the statue to Queen Victoria. Victoria, who died in 1901, epitomised the Empire. She was the Empress. It is little wonder that from his beginnings in Belfast at a time when Empire was still writ large and Emperors were commanding figures, Jack's early imaginative stories were set in India and that when we first meet Aslan in *The Lion, the Witch and the Wardrobe* he is described as the son of the Emperor over the sea.

The Linen Hall Library

The Linen Hall Library in Belfast is one of the few libraries in Ireland still funded by subscription from its private members and has among its collections a complete set of the work of C.S. Lewis. His father, Albert, was a subscribing member to the Linen Hall. At one point, Albert had political ambition and was interested in standing for a Westminster constituency. The Linen Hall

The Linen Hall Library

Library would have been in those times an invaluable resource for his research on a wide range of topics in an era that pre-dated the internet and was perhaps the only available source for some of the information he needed. Indeed it is still an invaluable source of information today, but for different reasons. The Linen Hall Library started its life as a reading room on the opposite side of the street in the old White Linen Hall where the City Hall now stands. Its move to Donegall Square North was necessitated by the demolition of the old Linen Hall in the year of Lewis's birth.

Little Lea

A blue plaque at Dundela Villas marks the location of C.S. Lewis's birthplace. A second blue plaque mounted on the house that later became the family home at 76 Circular Road marks the location where Jack spent his boyhood. The house is called Little Lea, probably because Albert essentially bought a small field (lea) on which to have it built. This house is of particular importance in the shaping of Lewis's early life. The family lived at Dundela until Easter 1905. Their first night in the new house was Good

Friday, 20 April 1905. Lewis tells us many things about the house and it was there, without doubt, that many of the important aspects of his life and work commenced. He tells us about the move to the house:

"In 1905 my seventh year, the first great event in my life took place. We moved house. My father growing I suppose in prosperity decided to leave the semi-detached villa in which I had been born and build himself a much larger house out in what was then the country" (6).

Little Lea showing plaque

By the time Lewis was writing about the move, he had observed that Belfast had continued its rapid growth and that between 1905 and 1955 when *SBJ* was published, Circular Road was no longer considered to be out in the country. Today it is simply a leafy suburb of East Belfast.

If anyone was to have any doubts as to the importance of the move to Little Lea, then Jack's own description of the event would dispel them. He says:

Plaque at Little Lea

"The new house is almost a major character in my story. I am a product of long corridors, empty sunlit rooms, upstair indoor silences, attics explored in solitude, distant noises of gurgling cisterns and pipes, and the noise of the wind under the tiles" (7).

In the paragraphs that follow in *SJB* he tells us graphically of life and living in that house and in those times. He tells us of "the view" from the front of the house for which the site had principally been chosen:

"From our front door we looked down over the wide fields to Belfast Lough and across it to the long mountain line of the Antrim shore – Divis, Colin, Cave Hill. This was in the far-off days when Britain was the world's carrier and the Lough was full of shipping; a delight to both of us boys but most of all to my brother. The sound of a steamer's horn at night still conjures up my whole boyhood" (8).

Following photo: Belfast Lough viewed from East Belfast

Little Lea

He recalls that while there were always people to talk to, mainly older people like his parents, his paternal grandfather who lived with them, the servants and the gardener, solitude was always within his reach in the garden but especially in the attics of the house. He tells us that very soon after moving to the new house he staked out a claim to the attics and it was here that he kept pen and ink. His first stories were written there and already the mood of the systematiser, redolent of Anthony Trollope in *The Barsetshire Chronicles*, was strong in Lewis. He tells us that his father enjoyed Trollope and indeed Jack himself at a later stage in life became an avid reader of Trollope. Most people are surprised to discover that Belfast celebrates an important link with Anthony Trollope. A blue plaque on the Custom House building marks the City's association with him where he was based in the offices of the Harbour Board when he worked in Belfast as the Post Office surveyor.

Lewis's grandfather, Richard Lewis, also worked for the Harbour Board after leaving the firm he founded on his arrival in Belfast so perhaps there should be two plaques on the Custom House building to mark associations with both of the notable personalities associated with the site. The stories written by Jack in the attics of Little Lea in Belfast had to be adapted on his brother's return from boarding school. If the stories were to be of interest to both boys they had to have trains and ships. Lewis's first book, written in childhood, took its shape in the attics of Little Lea. The book was later published as *Boxen* and tells the story of chivalrous mice and rabbits who rode out in complete chain mail not to kill giants, but cats!

This imagination that was born and at least in part cultivated in the attics of Little Lea developed into the mind that gave us *The Chronicles of Narnia*. It will not be lost on careful readers that the first of the books in the chronology of Narnia, *The Magician's Nephew*, starts with two children, Polly and Digory, in the attic of Uncle Andrew's house. The introduction to the Narnian Chronicle leaves the reader with no doubt that the author has had more than a passing familiarity with a childhood imagination stirred by the exploration of an attic. The attics first encountered by Lewis were the attics of Little Lea in Belfast.

His idyllic childhood continued for three unbroken years at Little Lea from 1905 to 1908. The holiday returns from boarding school of his brother Warren enriched the imaginative qualities of his untroubled existence until one February evening in the winter of 1908 that was to mark the beginning of a watershed experience in his Belfast boyhood. He describes it like this:

"There came an evening when I was sick with headache and toothache and distressed because my mother did not come to me" (9).

He tells us the reason for his mother's inability to come to him; she too was ill. A small medical team had arrived at their home on that day in February and after the necessary preparations, proceeded to perform major surgery to treat his mother's illness. Flora was operated on in the south dining room, on the kitchen table. She survived the surgery but ultimately not the illness.

It was cancer and she died some months later on 23 August 1908, Albert's birthday.   Lewis tells us of those months between February and August. He prayed for her recovery but gradually he saw her less and less as her condition deteriorated. The medics looked after Flora more and more and almost became a barrier between her and the children. Morphine cushioned her interface with reality and with her family. Jack's father did not cope well with the illness nor ultimately with the bereavement. He did not cope well with

Little Lea dining room window

helping the boys through this difficult time and with Flora's passing, the boys essentially lost both parents. Jack remembered the quotation on the calendar in her bedroom on the day that she died. The words were written indelibly in his mind and over fifty years later these same words that he first encountered in Little Lea in Belfast, were inscribed on his gravestone in Oxford (see Chapter 4).

It was a difficult August for the Lewis family. Albert lost his father, one of his brothers and his wife all in a matter of weeks. These experiences, but mostly the experience of his mother's illness, brought Jack face to face with his first memorable encounter with pain and suffering. For him it was a beginning of asking questions about why there should be pain and suffering in our world and some thirty years after these events he would attempt some answers in his

Inscription: Flora Augusta, wife of A. J. Lewis Little Lea, Strandtown. Died 23rd August 1908 aged 46

important book, *The Problem of Pain*. The genesis of the book can be traced to his early experiences at Little Lea.

This episode in the family life in Belfast was a turning point. The happy days he had spent in the family home and with his parents and Warnie came to a swift end. Within a matter of weeks from his mother's passing he had commenced a new chapter of his life which took on a very different pattern. By September he was travelling in the company of his brother to a boarding school in England just weeks after his mother's death. This whole experience of school and living away from home was new to him and he found it daunting. He describes a fairly melancholy departure from Little Lea in a "four-wheeler", a horse-drawn carriage, and the journey through a damp September twilight over the cobbled streets of an autumn Belfast to Donegall Quay where the boys would board the morning ferry to Fleetwood in Lancashire. The 'beginnings' in Belfast were approaching a gradual end.

Glenmachan

Close to the family home in Belfast was Glenmachan, a large house about a mile from Little Lea which was the home of the Ewart family. Sir William Ewart had partly financed the building of St Mark's Church and after his death, his son, Sir William Quartis Ewart, financed the completion of the sanctuary and the side chapels to the east end of the church. Jack's mother, Flora, had a cousin, Mary Elizabeth Heard, daughter of Robert and Charlotte Heard, who had married Sir William Quartis Ewart. Flora regarded Mary not only as her closest cousin but her best friend. After Flora's untimely death, cousin Mary took a real interest in the Lewis boys. They were invited regularly when they were in Belfast to dine at Glenmachan and to attend social functions there. The house was larger than Little Lea.

Glenmachan Tower, close to the former home of the Ewart family

Campbell College

Lewis describes it as the largest house he knew and he records fond memories of visiting there. One of the early photographs we have of C.S. Lewis as a child was taken at the Ewart home in Glenmachan. It was there that his social skills were refined and he attributes the positive effect on his manners to the efforts of Lady Ewart.

Campbell College

Lewis's initial schooling in England proved to be an educational disaster. In spite of the fact that Albert researched thoroughly all the possibilities for the education of his sons, Jack records for us his view that though his father's research was diligent, he proceeded to make all the wrong choices. Warnie seems to have coped with the situation better than Jack, but after much pleading in the letters written by Jack to his father, Albert finally made arrangements for Jack's education to be continued at Campbell College, Belfast, a boarding school close to Little Lea. In *SBJ* he records his unbridled

War memorial in Campbell College recording Lewis's name

enchantment at the prospect of returning to Belfast and attending Campbell
on a permanent basis. He writes:

"I did not believe that anything Irish could be bad, even a school"(10)

and to Campbell he accordingly went. It
was a short-lived experience, for during
the first term he became unwell and
although the illness was not particularly
serious he had to remain at home for some
weeks after which his father made new
arrangements for schooling to be resumed
at a different school in England. This

Names of C.S. Lewis and his cousin Richard

became the pattern of the rest of his schooldays until he became the private
pupil of W.T. Kirkpatrick, the Belfast schoolmaster, in preparation for Oxford
where he studied as an undergraduate after the end of World War I.

Former site of the McNeill family home

A short distance down the road from
Campbell College was the home of
the McNeill family.   J.A. McNeill first
impacts on the Lewis story through
his encounter with Flora who began
her education at Methodist College in
Belfast where McNeill was a teacher. The
McNeill family moved to East Belfast
when McNeill became headmaster at Campbell College. Janie McNeill,
daughter of J.A. McNeill, became a personal friend of young Lewis. Their
friendship was continued mainly through correspondence right up until Janie
died in 1959. Lewis wrote her obituary which was published in the school
magazine of Campbell College.

T. Edens Osborne

The year 1913 was a significant year in Lewis's life. He
describes it as a renaissance or reawakening of some of
the desires he had experienced in childhood. The stab
of 'JOY' he first experienced in the garden of the house in
Dundela Avenue where he was born, was reawakened

Adjacent house in the style of Lisnadene, 191 Belmont Road, Belfast

with his experience of 'Northernness'. This came initially through his reading a headline in a catalogue or in a literary supplement. The headline was 'Seigfried and the Twilight of the Gods'. Northernness engulfed him and again he experienced this sensation of 'JOY' or desire. Up to this point in his life he had not heard a note of Wagner's music but on return to Belfast for his summer holidays he wandered into a general merchant's shop in the city centre that sold phonographs and gramophones and there for the first time he heard being played in the shop *The Ride of the Valkyries*. Of that episode and an episode later that summer in the Dublin house of his Belfast cousins, the Ewarts, Lewis says:

"I cannot continue my story without noting... its bearing on the rest of my life". (11)

Period sales brochure of T Edens Osborne

The Belfast shop where Lewis first heard *The Ride of the Valkyries* was the shop of T. Edens Osborne in Wellington Place. It was this experience of Northernness and of his awakening interest in Norse myths and legends that was to lead him into two friendships that would become important in the development of the rest of his life. The two friendships were those with Arthur Greeves and J.R.R. Tolkien.

Arthur Greeves

On the other side of Circular Road from the Lewis's home, Little Lea, behind a high wooden fence stood a redbrick two storey house called Bernagh. The house is no longer there, having been demolished to make way for a development that has yet to take place. Bernagh was the home of the Greeves family. Joseph Malcolmson Greeves (the Malcolmson link was referred to in the introduction to Belfast) was a director of the Belfast firm of J. and T.M.

Location of Greeves family home, Circular Road

Greeves Ltd. The Greeves family had a flax-spinning business in Belfast and their mills were part of the linen industry that was driving the economy of Belfast in the late nineteenth and early twentieth centuries. It was in Bernagh that Lewis and Arthur Greeves, the son of Joseph Malcomson Greeves and Mary Margaretta Gribbon of New York, first met and began a lifelong correspondence that was to last for almost fifty years. Lewis records his first meeting with Arthur in the spring of 1914. Arthur had been unwell and had extended an invitation to Lewis to visit. It was during this visit that they discovered a common interest in the 'Myths of the Norsemen' and it was this interest in Norse mythology that was to commence a relationship that they sustained right up until Lewis died in 1963. It was in Arthur's house, Bernagh, on Circular Road in Belfast that Lewis wrote one of his first successful books. *The Pilgrim's Regress* was written by Lewis in the Greeves family home when he stayed there in 1931 during a visit to Belfast necessitated by his involvement in the winding up of his father's estate and selling Little Lea after his father died in 1929. Arthur provided Lewis with detailed editorial comment on the manuscript of *The Pilgrim's Regress* and Lewis records a dedication to Arthur at the front of the book. In a letter to Arthur dated 25 March 1933, Lewis writes with reference to the dedication that he proposed to include in the book:

Bernagh: Home of Arthur Greeves

"I suppose you have no objection to my dedicating the book to you? It is yours by every right – written in your house, read to you as written, and celebrating (at least in the most important parts) an experience that I have more in common with you than anyone else." (12)

The End of the Beginning

The events and environment of Lewis's early life undoubtedly gave to it an important shape that would mould his development. During his boyhood in Belfast his imagination was active and developing but he asks us to note that his imagination was never mistaken for belief. It was always distinct from reality and while he was aware of a desire that implied the absence of its object, he never confused imagination with belief. Lewis, writing about his early experiences of 'JOY' of desire and of imagination that first occurred in Belfast says that they are of such importance in understanding his early life that:

"the central story of my life is about nothing else". (13)

At the end of the summer term in 1913 he won a classical scholarship to Malvern College and the direction of his life continued on a trajectory that was shifting the locus away from Belfast to Oxford.

Following photo: C.S. Lewis at his desk in Oxford

Chapter Two
—— CORK, DUBLIN, BELFAST ——

BORN IN BELFAST

The opening chapter of this book presented details of the locations in Belfast
that are of significance in the life of C.S. Lewis and his family. While it focuses
on some of the WHERE questions, this chapter will attempt to pursue a number
of the HOW and WHAT questions. How did he come to be born in Belfast?
What were the circumstances that gave rise to his parents arriving in Belfast?
What other developments were beginning to occur at the end of the nineteenth
century that would be part of the landscape in the city around the time of his
birth and what was the history and fabric of his family that conspired to locate
his birth in Ulster? Most of the books written about Lewis have recorded
something of his genealogy and most have traced his ancestry, to some extent,
on both sides of his family. Indeed Lewis himself in *SBJ* tells us of the very

different backgrounds of his parents or "the
strains" that went into his making. In a few of the
opening sentences in *SBJ* he introduces us to his
Welsh ancestry through the Lewises on his father's
side and through his maternal grandmother
and her family, the Warrens. He sketches very
briefly his bloodline back to French roots via the
Normans and in particular to a Norman Knight,
William de Warne, who is buried at Battle Abbey
in Sussex. Lewis was conscious of his genealogical

Photo left: Cobh, Co Cork

Cobh, County Cork

background. He does make mention of a number of its details in the initial paragraphs of *SBJ* but makes few references to it elsewhere in his writing other than in passing. For him, it was by no means a major preoccupation. In one of the references he draws attention to the fact that although the Lewis and Warren lines are important in his background, his mother was a Hamilton. He says little more about the Hamilton line but this is a significant reference and one that should not be passed over in a record of his Belfast and Ulster origins. Many authors and Lewis enthusiasts have left on record significant detail of his genealogical background and some have referred to a few generations of the Hamilton line through which his ancestry runs. However, it is interesting to explore this line further back and the significance of his Hamilton link is highlighted later in this chapter.

Cobh railway station, now a heritage centre

The Lewises in Cork

The answer to the question, of how it came about that C.S. Lewis was born in Belfast, has its Irish beginnings in Cork, however, the family journey to Cork begins in Wales. The known history of the Lewis family goes back to 1775. His great–great–grandfather, Richard Lewis, was a farmer in Flintshire in north-east Wales.   The smallholding on which he raised his family was near Caergwrle, not far from modern-day Wrexham and close to the border with England. Richard had four sons and his fourth son, Joseph, left Caergwrle to move across the English border to Saltney, a suburb of Chester. Joseph had a family of eight. His fourth son, also called Richard, took an interest in engineering and, in particular, marine engineering. In 1853 he married Martha Gee and together they moved to Cork in Southern Ireland. Cork was at that time an important deep-water port and Richard Lewis went there to work as a master boilermaker with the Cork Steamship Company. Within eleven years of their move, all of their six children were born and Albert Lewis, C.S. Lewis's father, was born in Cork in 1863. In 1864 the family moved from Cork to Dublin. This was not the only significant family development that was taking place in Cork at this time and we will pick up what was happening to the Hamiltons in the same period in subsequent paragraphs.

Inside Cobh railway station

Cork to Dublin

Richard moved with his family from Cork
to Dublin to work with Walpole Webb and
Bewley, another company involved in shipping
and ship repair, in which Richard took a
job and worked as a manager. Although
the company is no longer in existence, the
Bewley name is still associated with a popular
brand of coffee widely available in Ireland
and with a major hotel chain. The company's
involvement in the importing of tea and coffee

Bewley's Hotel, Dublin

created an opportunity for Richard Lewis to work with them in the repair of
the ships needed by their business. It was there in the employment of Walpole
Webb and Bewley in Dublin that Richard met a man from Belfast called John H.
MacIlwaine and together they agreed to set up in business on their own account.
They decided, however, that they would not establish their business in Dublin but

Hamilton Road

would move to Belfast. This was a far-sighted and
entrepreneurial decision probably more comfortable
for John MacIlwaine who was from Belfast than for
the Lewises who were only recent arrivals in Ireland.
In 1868 they moved from Dublin to Belfast and the
Lewises set up home initially in the Mountpottinger
area of Belfast. It was shipbuilding that brought the
Lewises to Belfast and so shipbuilding more than
any other single influence is responsible for fixing
Belfast as the place of Lewis's birth. Richard Lewis's

business was registered as Lewis and MacIlwaine, Boilermakers, Engineers and
Iron Shipbuilders located just off Hamilton Road in the harbour area of the City,
now known as Titanic Quarter. Their business was just yards from the *Titanic*
Signature project that today occupies a prominent location on Belfast's waterfront

Hamilton road: fading sign

built as part of the celebration of the maritime
history of the city and the story of the building of the
Titanic. This is an interesting detail in itself because
of the association of Belfast with the construction of
Titanic, arguably the most famous ship in the world.

The *Titanic* Signature Project, Belfast

Titanic

Lewis and MacIlwaine set up their shipbuilding business in 1868 only a few hundred yards from the slipways where the famous *RMS Titanic* was built. The story of the construction and ultimate loss of this famous ship that was built in Belfast is known all over the world; its name having become almost synonymous with all that is grand, luxurious and huge as well as tragic. It is a lesser known story that two ships were built in Belfast with the name *Titanic* but the story of the other *Titanic* is directly relevant to the subject of this book because it was Lewis and MacIlwaine, Boilermakers, Engineers and Iron Shipbuilders that built the first *Titanic* in Belfast. This vessel was a more modest and utilitarian antecedent than its greater namesake but it was built by the company started by C.S. Lewis's grandfather, Richard. The vessel itself was a ship of 1608 gross tons, commissioned by H.J. Scott and Company of Ravenhill Road, Belfast, for the purpose of carrying freight from Glasgow

Citi Bank, Belfast location of Lewis and MacIlwaine business

to Belfast. For a time, the ship was operated by the Ulidia Navigation Company before it was sold on to a South American company, Cia de Lota y Coronel of Valparaiso in Chile and renamed the *Luis Alberto*. In 1915 the name of the ship was changed again, this time to the *Don Alberto* and finally the name was removed from the Lloyd's register of shipping in 1928, long after the second *Titanic* had been built and as it turned out, lost on her maiden voyage to New York. The first *Titanic* had a long and productive career - it served well, never sank, was not associated with major tragedy and so it passed into history almost unnoticed. Although its construction, launch and service were not noted particularly or celebrated on any large scale, nevertheless, it is part of Belfast's maritime history and its association with the Lewis family now means that it will remain as an interesting, almost coincidental sideshow to the place in history that has been carved out by the tragedy associated with its larger namesake.

Richard Lewis moved with his family from their initial home in the Mountpottinger area in Belfast to a house on Parkgate Avenue in East Belfast. The house is called Ty-isa and it is still there although much has changed in its surroundings. In travelling along Parkgate Avenue, the house is well hidden

SS Titanic built by Lewis and MacIlwaine 1888 Belfast. *Titanic: A Journey Through Time* by Eaton and Hass.

from view due to more recent development and unless its location is pointed out it can be missed easily. It is hardly surprising that the name of the house is Welsh, given Richard's Welsh roots. There is some discussion among Welsh speakers as to the meaning of Ty-isa, some of them emphasising the notion in the word that conveys the meaning of a house standing on its own, which is slightly ironic given the fact that it is today totally surrounded by other smaller houses. The alternative interpretation is that the name means "the low house" or the "lower house."

Whatever the meaning, the name of the house was Richard's last remaining link to the land of his fathers. He never returned to Wales, remaining in Belfast until his death in 1908. It was from Ty-isa that he travelled to work every day at Lewis and MacIwaine until he parted with the company to go and work with the Belfast Harbour Board. We know from copies of his letters that his initial salary with the Harbour Board was £150 per annum. The

Ty-isa , Parkgate Avenue, Belfast

Harbour Board offices were initially located at the site now occupied by the Custom House Building at Custom House Square before the Board was renamed and reconstituted as the Harbour Commissioners and moved to new, purpose-built accommodation at the impressive Harbour Commissioners' Building on Donegall Quay where Richard worked until his retirement. In his final years, Richard went to live at Little Lea with his son Albert, his grandsons Clive and Warnie and with his daughter-in-law who tragically also died in 1908, a disastrous year for the Lewis family and for Albert especially. It was from Ty-isa that Albert, C.S. Lewis's father, was sent to Lurgan College, a boarding school in County Armagh, where he was to meet W.T. Kirkpatrick, a figure who becomes very influential in his story.

Following photo: Belfast Harbour Commissioners' Building, Belfast

W.T. Kirkpatrick – An Ulster-Scot

Around the time that the Lewises were migrating northward to Belfast from Dublin, another family was resident in Belfast that would have a significant impact on the Lewis family and on C.S. Lewis in particular. The Kirkpatrick family had settled in Eliza Street in the Markets area of the City. This was a vibrant hub that saw the development of what is now St George's Market but also of small industrial businesses that

W.T. Kirkpatrick portrait in Lurgan College

later became significant in Belfast's shipbuilding empire.   It was in Eliza Street that Robert Hickson established his ironworks which was under the management of the young Edward Harland. This business was to evolve, merge and grow to become in a matter of a few years the mighty Harland

Eliza Street, Belfast

& Wolff. The Kirkpatrick family also had its base in Eliza Street. William T. Kirkpatrick was born in 1848 and was sent to school at the Royal Belfast Academical Institution or more simply 'Inst' as it is known in Belfast. The school was built in 1810 and served as a liberal Presbyterian school for boys which Kirkpatrick attended as a pupil and later became a teacher in the English Department of the school from 1868. In that same year he entered Assembly's College Belfast to train for ministry in the Presbyterian Church and although Kirkpatrick completed the academic requirements for ordination he was never ordained. By all accounts he was an impressive, forceful individual and an inspiring if slightly eccentric teacher.

St George's Market, Belfast

Kirkpatrick became headmaster of Lurgan College in 1876 where he remained until his retirement in 1899. It was in Lurgan College, County Armagh, that Albert Lewis first encountered Kirkpatrick, nicknamed 'the Great Knock'. Kirkpatrick was the headmaster at the school when Albert attended as a boy and it was through Kirkpatrick's influence that Albert was directed towards the legal profession as a career. After his retirement in 1899, Kirkpatrick moved to Great Bookham in Surrey and it was there in 1913 that he became private tutor to Warren Lewis and later from 1914 to 1917 he was private tutor to C.S. Lewis. Lewis, in his book *Miracles*, records a glowing tribute to this Belfast teacher for honing his mind and teaching him to think:

Union Theological College, Belfast

"The very man who taught me to think – a hard, satirical atheist (ex-Presbyterian) who doted on the Golden Bough *and filled his house with the products of the Rationalist Press Association – thought in the same way; and he was a man as honest as the daylight, to whom I here acknowledge an immense debt." (1)*

Walter Hooper asserts that the character of Macfee in Lewis's books *That Hideous Strength* and the *Dark Tower* was based on Kirkpatrick and there are echoes of Kirkpatrick in Digory Kirk who appears in *The Magician's Nephew*. It is Digory who is the subject of the famous sculpture in Belfast by Ross Wilson.

RBAI Belfast

Kirkpatrick was a major influence on young C S Lewis during what is referred to in *SBJ* as the "Bookham period." Under Kirkpatrick's tuition, Lewis's educational development accelerated. Lewis enjoyed every minute of it. He responded to Kirkpatrick's sense of humour, his learning, but also his atheism. Lewis observed closely Kirkpatrick's opinions and rhetorical styles and noted that although he had largely abandoned the church, he had retained a form of Sunday observance. On a Sunday he was to be seen doing his gardening in a more respectable suit! Lewis records of Kirkpatrick in *SBJ*.

"An Ulster Scot may come to disbelieve in God, but not to wear his week-day clothes on the Sabbath". (2)

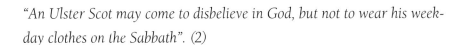
Lurgan College

Village road sign

Kilmacrenan village

Old graveyard at Kilmacrenan

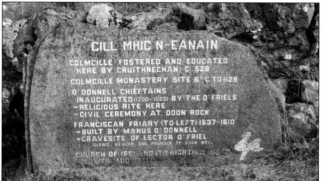

Marker stone for old Kilmacrenan Church of Ireland

Ruins of old Kilmacrenan Church of Ireland

Introducing the Hamiltons

C.S. Lewis's mother was Flora Hamilton, the youngest child of the Reverend Thomas R. Hamilton and his wife Mary (née Warren). Flora had two older brothers and a sister, Lilian. It seems that Lilian and Cecil were favoured by their parents and in consequence Flora and the younger of the boys, Gussy (Augustus Warren), formed a childhood alliance that lasted into adulthood. Florence was born in Queenstown, County Cork, on 18 May, 1862. Queenstown was known as Cobh (the Irish for Cove) until 1849 when the name of the town was changed in honour of the visit of Queen Victoria to Ireland. The Queen's Colleges in Belfast, Cork and Galway were also established at this time. After the partitioning of Ireland, Cobh reverted to its original name by which it is still known today. Flora's father, Thomas R. Hamilton, was the third in a consecutive line of Hamilton churchmen stretching back to 1729. His great-grandfather, Bishop Hugh Hamilton was born in 1729 and by 1764 was the Rector of the Church of Ireland church in Kilmacrenan in County Donegal. By 1768 he was Dean of Armagh and it was there that his son, also called Hugh, was born in 1790. Hugh and his family moved to Clonfert in County Galway where he was appointed as Bishop in 1796. Three years later they had moved to Kilkenny where Hugh concluded his career as Bishop of Ossory. His son Hugh II, who married Elizabeth Staples (from where C.S. Lewis inherited his second Christian name), became Rector of the Parish of Benmore and Inishmacsaint in County Fermanagh in 1824. Two years after taking up this appointment his son Thomas, grandfather of C.S. Lewis, was born in 1826. Lewis's grandfather was born in Ulster and on completion of his

Inishmacsaint Parish Church

studies at Trinity College in Dublin he returned in 1849 to Inishmacsaint as the curate. It is interesting that he was installed as curate during the period when his father was still the Rector. Thomas Hamilton was ordained in 1853 and served as a chaplain in the Royal Navy. He married Mary Warren in 1859 and in 1862 they moved to Queenstown, an important naval base where the last of their children, Florence Augusta, was born on 18 May, 1862.

Following photo: West doorway of ancient church at Clonfert

At this point we reach an interesting ganglion
in the unfolding story of C.S. Lewis and
his family. His father and mother with
their respective families, the Lewises and
the Hamiltons, are domiciled in Cork in
southern Ireland at precisely the same time
and both lived there for an overlapping
period of some six years. This coincidence
poses some interesting questions as to their
possible contact there. Even if the records do
not identify any specific contact between the
families, the births of Albert and Flora in Cork
and the shared period when they both lived
there would for certain have been a useful

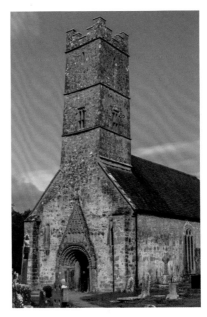

Clonfert Church

conversation starter when they would meet again in Belfast a decade later.

Both families left Cork after a relatively short stay. The Lewises left to go
ultimately to Belfast in 1868 in pursuit of a business in shipbuilding and
the Hamiltons in 1870 to go to Rome where Thomas, Flora's father, took up
the post of Curate in Holy Trinity Church. This venture to Italy was not the
first visit to continental Europe undertaken by Thomas Hamilton. He had
been before on the grand tour undertaken after his studies at Trinity College
in Dublin. It was this tour and the association with Italy that was probably
responsible for the selection of his youngest daughter's name, Florence.

St Canice's Cathedral, Kilkenny

The Hamiltons in Italy

C.S. Lewis was never in Italy. His interest in the language probably stems from the early tuition in Latin that he received in Belfast from his mother. She, as a slim, fair-haired girl with pale blue eyes, spent four years of her life

Grave of Bishop Hugh Hamilton, St Canice's

growing up in Rome before her family left Italy to travel to Belfast in 1874 when she was 12 years of age. It is important to record these details of the Hamilton family's route to Belfast which was where Flora settled, married and spent the remainder of her relatively short life; it is important because of the significance of the Italian interlude which gave Flora not only her love for languages but also the experiences she gained there with her family. These experiences would be talked about by the family many years later when they arrived in Belfast and not only talked about but listened to by the next generation, including the young C.S. Lewis. It requires little imagination to envisage the situation where the Hamiltons at some point in their four-year stay in Rome would have taken an excursion to Florence.

Headstone at Hugh Hamilton's grave

The link with her name alone would have been reason enough to undertake such a trip and also to add sufficient colour to the visit for it to become forever imprinted on her mind. In rehearsing the details of the visit to young Lewis, it is more than probable that the journey from Rome to Florence was commented on, perhaps only in passing, but nevertheless important because it was a journey that would have taken them through 'Narni', then a small town about halfway between Rome and Florence. Where did C.S. Lewis first hear the name of a place that sounded so like Narnia? Probably in Belfast, and probably from his mother, whose memory he cherished and possibly in a conversation between Flora and her parents or other family members for whom the visit to Narni was a lasting memory.

Florence in Belfast

Flora at twelve years of age left Rome with her family and moved to live in Belfast. For her father it was a return to Ulster where he had been born. He was returning in 1874 to become the Rector of St Mark's, Dundela, a parish on the eastern outskirts of the industrial city of Belfast. The congregation at Dundela had embarked on the project of erecting a new church which was opened in 1878 where the Reverend Thomas R. Hamilton was installed as the first Rector of the new church. For Flora it was a journey to the northern part of the island of her birth, and to what would be the birthplace of her sons some twenty years later. While it was shipbuilding that directed the Lewises to Belfast, it was the church that propelled the Hamiltons. The family moved into the new rectory adjacent to the church on the Holywood Road and Flora lived there as a teenager and until her marriage to Albert Lewis in 1894. By very different routes both families had left Cork and arrived in Belfast bringing Albert and Flora to within a mile of each other. The Rectory at St Mark's is only a few minutes' walk from the house with the Welsh name, Ty-isa, at Parkgate Avenue and the scene was set for the marriage of Albert Lewis, a Belfast solicitor to Flora Hamilton, the clergyman's daughter. The two strains that had both been in Cork in the 1860s went their separate ways, but had finally made their way to Belfast where C.S. Lewis and his brother Warnie were born of Lewis-Hamilton stock before the close of the century. In her teenage years, Flora commenced the formal part of her education. While Albert was being educated at Lurgan College, in County Armagh under the guidance of W.T. Kirkpatrick, Flora attended Methodist College, Belfast where

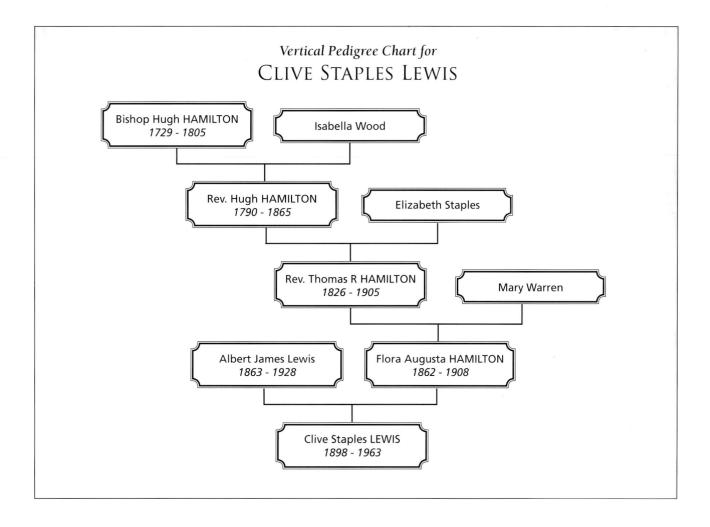

Vertical Pedigree Chart for
CLIVE STAPLES LEWIS

Bishop Hugh HAMILTON
1729 - 1805

Isabella Wood

Rev. Hugh HAMILTON
1790 - 1865

Elizabeth Staples

Rev. Thomas R HAMILTON
1826 - 1905

Mary Warren

Albert James Lewis
1863 - 1928

Flora Augusta HAMILTON
1862 - 1908

Clive Staples LEWIS
1898 - 1963

Methodist College, Belfast

she encountered J.A. McNeill, a mathematics teacher at the school. Flora attended 'ladies' classes' at Methodist College and whatever part, if any at all, played by J.A. McNeill in developing her interest, Flora pursued an interest in mathematics. She and her brother Gussie shared this interest and both demonstrated some mathematical ability and aptitude. The twists of fate determined that Gussie (Hamilton) commenced an apprenticeship in engineering with Lewis and MacIlwaine, Boilermakers, Engineers and Iron Shipbuilders of Hamilton Road in Belfast while Flora progressed to Queen's College, now Queen's University, Belfast. Queen's was then federated to the Royal Colleges of Ireland and there in 1886 after gaining double honours in mathematics and logic, Flora completed her BA degree, one of the few women among the students graduating in that year. Her teacher J.A. McNeill left Methodist College in 1890 and moved to live in East Belfast at a house called Lisnadene at 191 Belmont Road. The move to East Belfast was because of his taking up the post of headmaster at Campbell College, the Belfast school that C.S. Lewis was to attend for a short time in 1910. Athough J.A. McNeill had died in 1907, his daughter Jane Agnes McNeill (Janie) became a lifelong associate of C.S. Lewis. Lisnadene was just a short walk from Belmont Presbyterian Church which the McNeills attended and from Little Lea, the boyhood home of C.S. Lewis. Lisnadene is no longer on the site at 191 Belmont but the adjacent house provides some idea of what it was like. Lewis dedicated the third in his science fiction trilogy, *That Hideous Strength*, to Janie, a gesture she may not have entirely appreciated given the image conjured up by the title. He also wrote her obituary which was published in the *Victorian*, the magazine of Victoria College, the school she attended and in the *Campbellian*, the school magazine of Campbell College.

Archway at Queen's showing 1884 date

The House of Hamilton

The first part of this chapter outlined how Lewis came to be born in Belfast and the "strains" that were in his making. Specific references to his maternal grandparents, the Hamiltons, have been detailed. Little has been published by other Lewis commentators on the significance of the Hamilton name to the island of Lewis's birth but to anyone with any knowledge or interest in the political landscape of Ireland and of Ulster in particular, the name Hamilton will have a definite resonance.

1884 when C.S. Lewis's mother attended
Queen's College Belfast

Following photo: Church of Ireland Cathedral, Armagh

A little reflection on this branch of his family will help to position Lewis with reference to the Ulster-Scots tradition that is important in the understanding of present-day Northern Ireland. There are several of his ancestors that merit comment to highlight Lewis's Ulster-Scots lineage and the significance of that link to the island of his birth.

Armagh to Killyleagh

In the previous paragraphs, Lewis's maternal grandfathers were referenced taking the line back to his great-great-grandfather Hugh Hamilton, Bishop

Trinity College, Dublin

of Ossory. Hugh Hamilton was born in 1729 and is an interesting ancestor in the genealogy of C.S. Lewis. As a young man Hugh studied at Trinity College, Dublin and was a Fellow of Trinity in 1751. He became Professor of Natural History in 1759 and his writing embraced subjects as diverse as mathematics, the natural sciences and religion. Hugh ultimately inherited the estates of his father Alexander Hamilton in Armagh and entered the church, becoming Dean of Armagh in 1768. He married Isabella Wood, daughter of Hans Widman Wood and the first of their family was born at Armagh. After serving as Dean of Armagh, Hugh was appointed as Bishop of Clonfert in County Galway and towards the end of his career was translated to the see of Ossory. His tombstone is adjacent to the cathedral in Kilkenny. Hugh is interesting in terms of his learning and his writing. Given his mathematical, scientific and religious interests it is not difficult to recognise these traits and abilities in the family line, one of whom would eventually marry into the

Lewis family and become the mother of Jack and Warnie Lewis. However, going back the other way leads us through interesting times in the history of Ireland and to notable ancestors of C.S. Lewis that precede Hugh of Ossory. Hugh's father is an interesting and important link in the ancestral chain because of his family's significance in the Balbriggan story, the story of Hampton Hall and of the resulting Hamworth tradition.

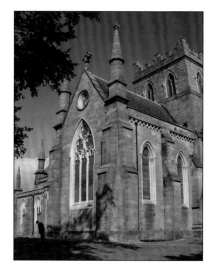

Armagh Cathedral

Balbriggan

Balbriggan harbour

Balbriggan shoreline

Balbriggan lighthouse built by the Hamiltons

Balbriggan

Hugh Hamilton (Ossory) was the eldest son of Alexander Hamilton, styled at various points as Alexander of Killyleagh and Knock. Killyleagh (spelled today with a y but variously in documents from the 1600s on) is a small village in County Down in Northern Ireland and Knock is in County Dublin. Alexander was an imminent solicitor and became the Member of Parliament (MP) for Killyleagh during the years 1730 - 1759. In 1736 Alexander greatly extended the family lands by purchasing from Robert Kiernan an area known as little Balbriggan just north of Dublin and fifteen years later he added to this another 172 acres which were skilfully developed, cultivated and some of it leased. At the Balbriggan estate he commenced the building of Hampton Hall which was completed in 1758, the year before he died. With the exception of Alexander's son, Bishop Hugh, who entered the church, the rest of the family remained in Balbriggan developing the harbour, St George's Church and a cottage industry in cotton and fabrics. Several members of the family are interred in the family vault at Balrothery. The family estates at Balbriggan began to incur significant debts in the years following the death of Alexander

Hamilton and a process of selling off the assets began. The harbour which required to be dredged continually was eventually transferred to the authority of the Dublin Port and Docks Board, some of the land was sold to the Dublin and Drogheda Railway Company and other lands were variously mortgaged to distant family members. In Ireland generally, times grew increasingly difficult in the early nineteenth century and members of Alexander Hamilton's family became involved in the Relief Committees established to provide assistance to families affected by the disastrous famine caused by the failure of the potato crop in 1845. Hampton Hall itself passed out of the ownership of the descendants of Alexander Hamilton. It was sold to a succession of families and in 1998, one hundred years after the birth of C.S. Lewis, it was eventually bought by David Pratt of Skerries who lived there until his death in 2009. As well as refurbishing the ancestral Hamilton home in Balbriggan, David Pratt also documented its history. He commented generously on the succeeding generations of the family of Alexander Hamilton that had its beginnings at a small farm at Knock, Balrothery, County Dublin, and that did so much for the development of a tiny fishing village on the east coast of Ireland. Charles Hamilton, son of Alexander and brother of C.S. Lewis's direct

Hampton Hall, Ballbriggan

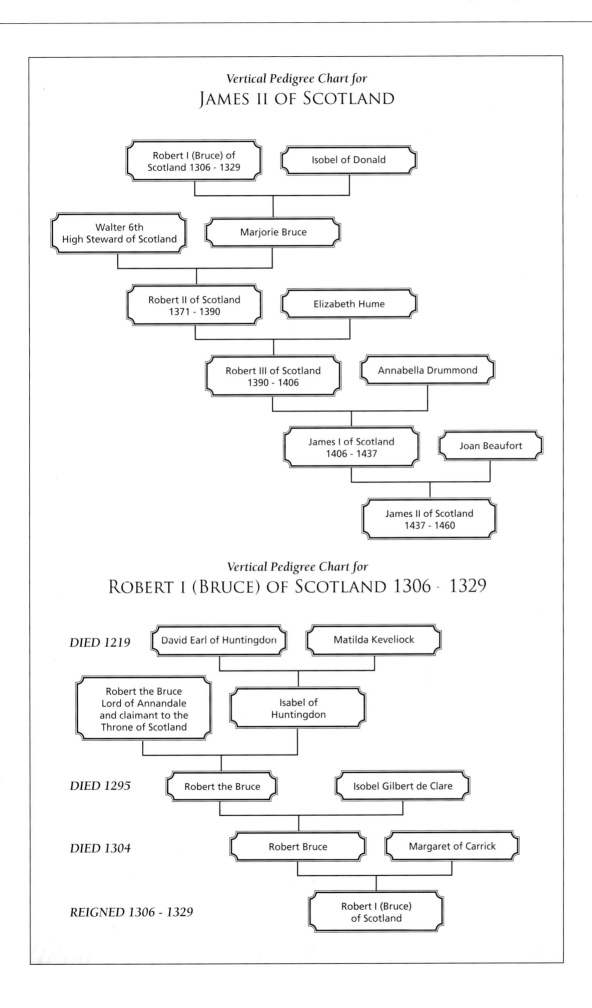

Vertical Pedigree Chart for
JAMES II OF SCOTLAND

Robert I (Bruce) of Scotland 1306 - 1329

Isobel of Donald

Walter 6th High Steward of Scotland

Marjorie Bruce

Robert II of Scotland 1371 - 1390

Elizabeth Hume

Robert III of Scotland 1390 - 1406

Annabella Drummond

James I of Scotland 1406 - 1437

Joan Beaufort

James II of Scotland 1437 - 1460

Vertical Pedigree Chart for
ROBERT I (BRUCE) OF SCOTLAND 1306 - 1329

DIED 1219   David Earl of Huntingdon   Matilda Keveliock

Robert the Bruce Lord of Annandale and claimant to the Throne of Scotland

Isabel of Huntingdon

DIED 1295   Robert the Bruce   Isobel Gilbert de Clare

DIED 1304   Robert Bruce   Margaret of Carrick

REIGNED 1306 - 1329   Robert I (Bruce) of Scotland

The Royal Line

Having traced the Hamilton line of Lewis's ancestors back to Fynnart in Renfrewshire, it is a short and secure step to Scottish royalty. James Hamilton of Fynnart, the natural son of James Hamilton, the first Earl of Arran and Mary Boyd, is directly descended from his grandfather James Hamilton, first Lord Hamilton of Cadzow who was born in 1426. Cadzow (pronounced Cadyow) was the area in Scotland now identified with the town of Hamilton in which Hamiltons, the first of the name, settled on their move north from Hambledon in Leicestershire, England. The first Lord of Cadzow married Mary Stewart and the first Earl of Arran was their eldest son. Mary Stewart was none other than Princess Mary Stewart, daughter of King James II of Scotland, a direct ancestor of C.S. Lewis. From James II of Scotland, it is a matter of record that is easily traced, to take the line back from James II of Scotland to the House of Bruce, to the famous Robert the Bruce, Lord of Annandale and to David, Earl of Huntingdon (1124) with a direct line back to the House of Alpin and to a daughter of William de Warrenne whom Lewis references in *Surprised by Joy* in the context of a different genealogical line that became the family of his maternal grandmother, Mary Warren, whose name comes from de Warrenne.

Killyleagh Castle (opposite page the entrance to the castle)

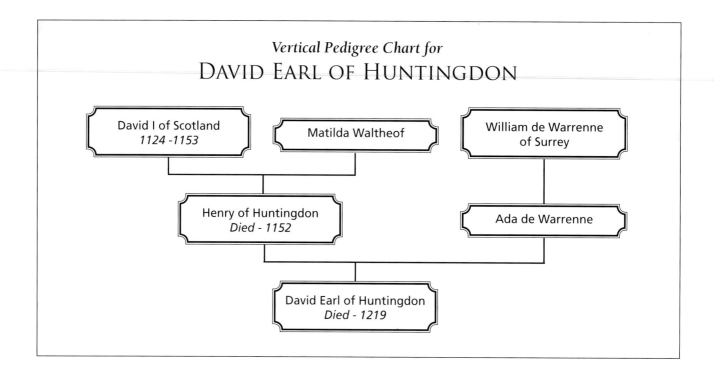

Vertical Pedigree Chart for
David Earl of Huntingdon

David I of Scotland *1124 -1153*	**Matilda Waltheof**

William de Warrenne of Surrey

Henry of Huntingdon *Died - 1152*

Ada de Warrenne

David Earl of Huntingdon *Died - 1219*

The Hamilton - Montgomery Settlement in Ireland (1606)

Reference was made above to the fact that to anyone in Ireland with an interest in the history of the island and of parts of Ulster in particular, the name Hamilton would have a resonance and in terms of genealogy the name would provoke interest. To complete the links of Lewis's ancestry to the island of his birth it is only necessary to deal with one more significant link. When the Hamilton line moved from Sir James of Fynnart across the Irish Sea with William and Hugh, the latter leased lands from a distant relative, Sir James Hamilton styled of Clandeboye and later Earl of Clanbrassil.

The Clanbrassil Story

Sir James was the son of a clergyman, Hans Hamilton of Dunlop in Scotland, and was the first of his family line to come to Ireland around 1587. James Hamilton first came to Ireland as a schoolmaster and when Queen Elizabeth I established Trinity College in Dublin, the first Provost of Trinity persuaded Hamilton and his fellow Scotsman, James Fullerton, to become Fellows at the College. Hamilton became bursar at Trinity and both men became agents of King James VI of Scotland. On the death of Elizabeth, James acceded to the throne of England as James I (and VI of Scotland) at the Union of the Crowns in 1603. The King rewarded Hamilton for his services by granting him extensive lands in Co Down along with a knighthood and the titles of Viscount Clandeboye and Earl of Clanbrassil.   In a separate and complex political manoeuvre, involving Hamilton along with Hugh Montgomery and Sir Phelim O'Neill, all three of whom were in favour at court with the King, Hamilton gained extensive lands formerly owned by O'Neill. What happened was that the O'Neills fell out of favour with the King, and Hugh Montgomery was contacted by Ellis O'Neill, wife of Con O'Neill, to ask him to secure the release of her son who was being held at Carrickfergus Castle. The release was secured by Montgomery on the understanding that on the granting of safe passage for the O'Neills to England, the lands held by O'Neill would transfer to Montgomery. The deal did not quite go according to plan. The King granted a pardon to the O'Neills but divided the O'Neill lands between Montgomery and Sir James Hamilton. It is interesting that the seat of the O'Neills was the Norman castle at Castlereagh formerly in the Castlereagh hills that C.S. Lewis could see from the home of his birth and that caused such a sense of longing in his childhood. His sense of *Sehnsucht* might have been enhanced had he known the history of Castlereagh and his interest, shared with J.R.R. Tolken, in Norse mythology may have gone deeper had he been aware of his ancestral links.

A final point in the ancestral line is worth making. Hans, the father of Sir James Hamilton, Earl of Clanbrassil, (from whom William and Hugh leased lands at Lisbane), died in Dunlop in Scotland and Sir James had a memorial erected at the church in Dunlop where his father is buried. This line of the Hamilton family in Scotland goes back through Hans's father, Archibald of Raploch, and back along the Raploch line which is descended from Sir John Hamilton (1370 - 1402) of Cadzow and

Clandeboye: part of the estates of Sir James Hamilton, Viscount Clandeboye

Jacoba Douglas, grandfather and grandmother of James Hamilton, the first. Lord Hamilton who married Mary Stewart. Thus it happens that Hugh of Lisbane is directly, if distantly, related to Sir James, Earl of Clanbrassil who is buried at Bangor Abbey in County Down. The Clanbrassil title passed to Sir James's son and the lack of a male heir in the next generation resulted in the titles falling into disuse.

Following photo: Carrickfergus Castle and Harbour, County Antrim

The Ewarts

There is another important branch of Lewis's relatives, the Ewarts, that is worth mentioning at this point before we consider a final comment by Lewis on the subject of family history. It is important to include his connection with the Ewart family for two reasons. Firstly, because the Ewarts were a significant part of the fabric of the Belfast into which Lewis was born and, secondly, because he includes a very specific reference to them in *SBJ*. This reference is in a section where he contrasts the characteristics of the Lewis relatives, mainly his uncle Joseph Lewis and his family who were cousins to Jack and Warnie, with the Hamiltons and in particular with his mother's brother Gussie for whom he had an enduring fondness. At the end of this reference to the Lewises and the Hamiltons he comments that there were other relatives who featured more prominently and for him more agreeably, than his aunts and uncles. A short distance from his boyhood home Little Lea was another house that forever remained in his memory. At the time of writing *SBJ* in 1955, Lewis uses the name 'Mountbracken' to refer to this house in an attempt to preserve its privacy. The matter is now of lesser consequence since the house is long gone. The fact is that the house was called Glenmachan and was then the largest house that Lewis knew when he was growing up in Belfast. The location is now marked by a more recent development of houses still called by the name Glenmachan and opposite the former Glenmachan Hotel, now a residential home for the elderly. Glenmachan was the home of the family of Sir William Quartis Ewart who was married to Mary Heard, a cousin of Flora Lewis, Jack's mother.

The Ewarts, mentioned above in Chapter 1 as being mill owners and part

of the linen barons of Belfast, were key players in the growth and development of the city's industrial base in the manufacture of linen. William Ewart and Sons along with other firms such as Malcolmson and Co and Greeves formed the core of Belfast's engagement in the linen industry that provided so much employment in the early part of the twentieth century. Sir William Ewart, who married Isabella Kelso, had contributed significantly to the cost of

building St Mark's Church of which C.S. Lewis's grandfather was the first
Rector. The east window in the church is in memory to Isabella, mother of
Sir William Quartis Ewart who married Mary Heard, a cousin of Flora Lewis
(née Hamilton). Mary was described by Flora not only as her closest cousin
but her dearest friend. After Flora's untimely death, it was Lady Mary who
extended a regular invitation to Albert, Jack and Warnie for Sunday lunch and
to visit Glenmachan for the numerous social events that were hosted by the
Ewarts. Lewis attributes the fact that he and his brother grew up in a civilised
fashion to the influence of Lady Mary and to the many invitations they

received to dine at Glenmachan. The interest in their
welfare Lewis says reflects the closeness of the bond of
friendship between his mother and Mary.

It was Sir William Quartis Ewart who provided
much of the financial support for the completion
of the transepts and chancel of St Mark's. The
commemorative panels in the south transept are in
memory of members of the Ewart Family.

Glenmachan Tower, Belfast

Lewis on Ancestry

What would Lewis have made of the links of his Ulster-Scots ancestors
with the island on which he was born? It is impossible to know. The fact
is that while he was aware of some of the ancestral detail of his maternal
grandmother's family, he made little or nothing of his genealogy on the
Hamilton side. Although his brother Warnie spent a considerable number of
years compiling and editing the Lewis papers that include some reference to
the Hamilton family, C.S. Lewis himself does not display a great knowledge,
interest or awareness of some of the detail. He deals with his family
background on all sides in a few paragraphs in *SBJ* and in the rest of his
writing he makes almost nothing of it at all. For those interested in Lewis's
contribution to literature, to philosophy and theology, the details of his
ancestral background and the location of his birth provide some additional
atmosphere to his story. It is also interesting to note that two of his earliest
publications *Spirits in Bondage* in 1919 and his long narrative poem 'Dymer'
1926 were not published under the name of C.S. Lewis but published under
the pseudonym of Clive Hamilton!

Inscription to William Quintis Ewart erected by his parents William Quartis Ewart and Mary Warren Ewart

In memory of Richard Ewart, son of Sir William Ewart. Died in New York 1918, interred at Lowell, Massachusetts USA

In memory of James Ewart, son of Sir William Ewart, died in New York 1898, interred at Sommerville, New Jersey, USA

On all of this we must give to Lewis himself the final word. In his book first published under the title of *Beyond Personality* and subsequently as Book IV of *Mere Christianity* he says in Chapter 5 when writing of human beings:

"They look separate because you see them walking about separately. But then, we are so made that we can see only the present moment. If we could see the past, then of course it would look different. For there was a time when every man was part of his mother, and (earlier still) part of his father as well and then they were part of his grandparents. If you could see humanity spread out in time, as God sees it, it would not look like a lot of separate things dotted about. It would look like a single growing thing — rather like a very complicated tree. Every individual would appear connected with every other." (3)

If we have done anything in pursuing Lewis's background in terms of the people and the island of his birth, we have illustrated the point he was making in *Beyond Personality*, we are all connected.

In Chapter 15 of *Prince Caspian*, there is a short section in the narrative where Lewis has Caspian commenting on his own ancestry. Caspian wishes in the story that he had come of more honourable lineage only to be reminded by Aslan that he has come from the Lord Adam and Lady Eve:

" ...and that is both an honour enough to erect the head of the poorest beggar, and to bow the shoulders of the greatest emperor on earth. Be content". (4)

'The Searcher' sculpture by Ross Wilson at Holywood Arches, Belfast

C.S. Lewis as a child: with all his road before him

Chapter Three
—The Counties of Ulster—

A Less Travelled Road

To say that Lewis was not a well-travelled man would be an accurate enough statement but it would not provide an adequate picture of the shape of his life. His travels beyond the United Kingdom and Ireland were indeed limited, even if memorable in his own experience. He recalls, but passes over briskly, a childhood holiday in Normandy during August 1907 with his mother and Warnie, describing it as leaving with him vivid memories but as an event of no account. In later life, after his retirement, and three years after his marriage to Joy Davidman, he and Joy travelled for a short holiday to Greece in April 1960. With these notable exceptions, along with his military service in France during 1917, Lewis's travelling was limited to the British Isles.

All My Road Before Me

Walter Hooper, one of the most notable of Lewis scholars, employs a phrase from Lewis's own narrative poem 'Dymer' as the title under which he published Lewis's diaries. The phrase occurs in the following short section of the poem:

Donegall Quay 2013

"You stranger, long before your glance can light
Upon these words, time will have washed away
The moment when I first took pen to write,
With all my road before me..." (1)

While the road Lewis travelled did not take him far and wide in geographical terms, his travels did begin early and they were frequent. Travelling between Belfast and various destinations in England was to become a characteristic of his way of life. From the age of nine, and almost immediately after his

mother's death, Lewis was sent to a number of boarding schools in England. At the beginning and end of each term, three times in each school year, the round trip between Belfast and school in England became part of his life.

The opening sentences of Chapter 2 in *SBJ* describe his memory of the first cross-channel journey to school in England. It was a dismal affair, travelling for the first part of the journey in a horse-drawn carriage over

Donegall Quay as Lewis would have seen it

the rough cobbled streets of Belfast on a wet autumn evening to board the ferry at Donegall Quay. He remembers the sound of the horse's hooves and the noise of the wheels on the road as the only sound breaking the silence that had descended gloomily over his father and brother. This was the first

of the numerous crossings to England that characterised his youth. He quickly became a seasoned traveller in comparison to the more normal and very limited travelling experiences of most children and many adults living in Ireland in the early 1900s. Partly because of the travelling, both Lewis boys felt quite sophisticated at an early stage in their lives and it was while travelling, especially between Belfast and England, that Lewis formulated some of his writing. While his physical journeys were within narrow geographical boundaries, his philosophical journeys, as he chronicled them in *The Pilgrim's Regress*, were wide ranging. It was during a number of his journeys that he read books that were significant, formative and memorable such as *Tamburlaine* which he first read en route from Larne to Belfast and George MacDonald's *Phantasties*.   Some of his writing such as *The Pilgrim's Regress* was formulated during his travels back to Belfast and many of his constant memories resulted from these journeys. He writes of these journeys in Chapter 10 of *Surprised by Joy*:

"You will understand that I had been crossing the Irish Sea six times a year since I was nine. That is why my memory is stored with ship's-side images to a degree unusual for such an untravelled man. I only have to close my eyes to see if I choose, and sometimes whether I choose or no, the phosphorescence of a ship's wash, the mast unmoving against the stars though the water is rushing past us, the long salmon-coloured rifts of dawn or sunset on the horizon of cold grey-green water or the astonishing behaviour of land as you approach it, the promontories that walk out to meet you, the complex movements and final disappearance of the mountains further inland." (2)

Ship's-side image of the current ferry from Belfast

View of Belfast from Cave Hill

Lewis's first interactions with the geography of his native Ulster were visually striking. Although he was born in Belfast and on the County Down side of the River Lagan, his daily view from the front of the house in which he was born was of the hills of County Antrim. This same view was the panorama of Divis Mountain, Colin and the Cave Hill, that was visible clearly from the house where he spent most of his childhood. In early boyhood, the Castlereagh Hills and the Hills of Down captured his imagination but his earliest travels were through County Antrim and to County Londonderry.

Ballycastle harbour

County Antrim

The earliest evidence of Lewis's travels to and through
County Antrim is contained in the letters written
by his mother, Flora. These record their summer
holidays of 1900 spent in the small seaside town of

Ballycastle perched on the northern coastline some seventy miles from
Belfast. Flora's letters in that year cover the period from June through until
August and indicate that they stayed at Quay Road, Ballycastle. The letters

contain references to "Baby" who at twenty months
was teething but also talking. Flora records in a letter
to Albert her surprise at the words "Babsie" was able
to put together. Whatever remained in his memory
of the holiday, his mother records that he said clearly
enough that he wanted to remain at Ballycastle and
that he was "not going home". Although he was only
an infant at this stage, and probably remembered little
of the holiday itself, Ballycastle remained a strong
image with the family. The humorous references to
"the promenade" written many years later in his own
hand on the flyleaf of the presentation copy of his
published poem, 'Dymer', given to his father, may refer
to the ice-cream shop of the same name on the main
street in Ballycastle.

Quay Road, Ballycastle where the Lewises stayed
for their holiday in summer 1900

The holiday of 1900 was the beginning of Lewis's
familiarity with the north coast. It was a place to
which he would return regularly throughout his life
and from sources such as his letters to Arthur Greeves,
it is clear that he wished to return more frequently
than was actually possible. Several batches of letters
contain details of visits planned, but abandoned for
a variety of reasons at the last minute. The powerful
images of the rugged coastline with its equally
dramatic history would find their way into and make
an impact on his writing.

The view from Quay Road, Ballycastle

Quay Road
Ballycastle

6 August 1900

My Dearest Al

I ought to have written to you yesterday but could not find a minute... I like the nice crisp feel in the air.

I met Mrs McDermott of Belmont: she comes here every year. I also saw Mr Cook and the Wakefield Dixons; so there are a good many Belfast people here. Your letter had not come by mid-day on Saturday, so I went up to the post (office) and found it lying there. They just said they did not know which house it was, so I pointed out that the house had neither name or number, and that they might have asked but of course they would not bother about it. However they say they will send it down in future. I hear that with the exception of the Fennel's, that house we were in has never been occupied since we were there.   I see that a grey house over-looking the links, which was being built when we were here is to let for September. I will have a look at it and find out the rent for a future occasion.

Babsie is talking like anything. He astonished me this morning: Warren sniffled and he turned round and said, "Warnie wipe nose". I suppose your mother and father will be home today; find out if the Larne people had any idea of coming here as if so I would write to them again.

Warren is greatly interested in the brick making which perhaps you may remember is carried on below the railway; he is always wanting to go there also there is a waterwheel which works a circular saw which is a great attraction..

Do you think of coming down before Saturday? It would be better to come when you can stay the night, it is really tiring to go back the same day. What about coming on Thursday and staying till Sunday or Monday? That would be nice, and if the weather was at all fine we could go for a drive.

I suppose you were not able to do anything about the Bangor house; perhaps if not let, the owner would let them have it for Sept. instead of August.

Good bye now, dear, with lots of love from your own wife

Flora

Quay Road
16 August 1900

My Dearest Bear

        I am sorry you are not coming down this week, but of course it is much
better to wait till the middle of the week and have more time with us; remember
Thursday will be the 23rd. you must try to get down for that. .....

The bathing dress came alright today, for which many thanks. I will try to get
a bathe tomorrow. It has been very hot since you left and it looks as if it was
going to stay fine for a while; we must have a drive next week either Thursday or
Friday. Saturday is a bad day to get a car,... I hear they have a nice little
open carriage at the Antrim Arms Hotel, it might suit us. I am all right again
now, so you must not worry about me. ..... Would Gussie come to come down to see
how his engine is going? Tell him we can put him up if he likes to come. .....
Babsie is not sleeping very well the last few nights; he is not cross, but wants
to get up and talk and play. I suppose it is the heat. He talks about his pappy
and wants to go and meet him when he goes out. ..... Now I must stop or miss this
post, so good bye for a short time

                                        Always your loving wife
                                        Flora

Ballycastle postbox

View of Ballycastle coastline from the end of Quay Road

                              Quay Road
                              Ballycastle
                              19 August 1900

My own dear Lal,

        I was expecting to hear from you yesterday, so I am
glad you did not wait for today to write, and though I am starting
my letter today, I have very little hope of being able to finish it
before five o'clock. You will understand the situation when I tell
you that it has rained ever since we got up, and that Martha went
to early church, so I have had the two of them on my hands all the
morning and off and on through the afternoon. ..... I suppose it
will be the 3:15 from Belfast on Thursday, same as last week. Now
do not let anything prevent you coming, I should be so much vexed,
and it will have time to clear up by them. ..... I have had two
lovely bathes and enjoyed it very much, we have had a lovely week
up to today , bright and fine.
.....

                              Always your own
                              Doli

                                        BallyCastle
                                        29 August 1900

My Dearest Lal

        I was at Castlerock, as we arranged, yesterday,
and found that Aunt H had gone to spend the day at Derry which
is only an hour by train from there, so I wrote her a note
asking her to come and spend today with me here, in answer
to which I have got the enclosed most unsatisfactory reply.
..... I went to the theatricals on 28th with the Hewitts. Mr
Montague was the husband and not the son of Mrs M. They say
that she is in Australia, and that he will not take her back
again.   He and all the children are living at Portstewart.

I suppose it will be all right about the engaged carriage on
Friday? I wrote to Tedford about the cabs. Babs says every
time we ask him, "not going home". He wants to stay here. We
have had a noisy day here with the fair; Badgie had several
rides. Did you remember that today was your wedding day?
..... I am sending this to the office on the chance that it
might not be in time for the morning delivery at Ty-isa.

                        Always you loving wife
                        Doli

The promenade at Ballycastle

Castlerock, County Londonderry

The letters from Flora to Albert indicate that the summer holidays of 1901 and 1904 were spent at Castlerock in County Londonderry. The journey from Belfast was undertaken by train which would have taken them through Coleraine to the small railway station in Castlerock.   This summer holiday is one that would stand out in young Lewis's memory.

Castlerock railway station

The letter dated 10 July 1901 indicates clearly that Lizzie, who was employed by the Lewises as the children's nurse, was with Flora and the children that summer. The weather that day was memorable because of an afternoon thunderstorm. Both of the children were frightened by the loud peals of thunder and Jack sat on Lizzie's knee hiding his face until the thunder passed. This reference to Lizzie was to Lizzie Endicot who is mentioned with great fondness by Lewis over fifty years later in *SBJ* as his childhood nurse in whom even the exacting memories of childhood could find no fault. It was with Lizzie that he shared a joke that could not be shared in the drawing room with the other significant adults in his life and it is likely that it was because of Lizzie and her fondness for a train driver called Jack that C.S. Lewis became known for a lifetime to his family, friends and colleagues as Jack Lewis.

Castlerock station and crossing

The 1904 letters identify the address where they stayed as Clifton Terrace, Castlerock, and from the detail in one of the letters it is clear that the bedroom occupied by the boys looked directly out on the railway line. Jack's childhood fascination with trains is recorded by his mother in her letters of that year. In one of the small shops in Castlerock she bought him a little wooden train and he refused to pass the railway tracks if the signal indicated that a train was expected. On that summer holiday Flora's letters record that Jack became a great friend of the stationmaster whom he greeted cordially when he was sent on an errand to buy the daily paper in a local shop.

Jack's bedroom window overlooked the railway line and from their arrival at Clifton Terrace he and Warnie were up early looking out to see the trains passing on the Castlerock to Derry line.

Castlerock to Londonderry railway station as seen from the rear of Clifton Terrace

In the letters, reference is made to a planned day trip by train to Derry towards the end of the holiday in August 1904 to see the famous and historical walls of the City and the old cannons that still form part of the walls today.

Clifton Terrace is still standing on the site it occupied in 1904 where Lewis spent his childhood holidays. The house itself has an interesting history. It was built during a period when the MP for the area, Sir Henry Hervy Bruce, who had inherited the Downhill House, lands and title, was Chairman of Londonderry's first County Council. He took a particular interest in the quality of the buildings that were being developed in the village and Clifton Terrace, where the Lewises stayed, was one of these. Sir Henry married Marianne Clifton, the daughter of a wealthy Nottinghamshire family and ultimately inherited the Clifton Estates in England. Undoubtedly, Clifton Terrace derives its name from the family name of Lady Marianne Clifton. Sir Henry and Lady Marianne are buried in the Bruce mausoleum in Dunboe graveyard, located on the main road from Castlerock to Downhill.

Clifton Terrace, Castlerock

Bath Villa

Castlerock

Friday June 1901

My Dearest Lal

        We got down comfortably last night. Babbins was delighted with the
train .....   We found our grocery things and milk in the house , so we were about
to get our teas comfortably. .....   Babs did not wake up till 9:30 so I suppose he
was tired with his journey. The Sea down here is lovely. The drawing room and the
dining room and two bed rooms look out on it.   Badge is quite delighted with it
and takes the greatest pleasure in watching the waves; they are both down on the
sand all the morning, baby much concerned because he can't manage to find a crab;
also he is very anxious to go into the water, hut I can't let him till his cough
is a bit better. I had a bathe before breakfast; it is very salt water and makes
you all tickley, so I doubt if it would suit you. ..... Lizzie is delighted with
the place, and has brought her bathing dress; ..... How did you get on down at
Bangor? .....

                                        Always you loving wife,

                                        Flora

                                        Bath Villa
                                        10 June 1901

My Dearest Lal,

..... I have been all right since I got over the journey headache, only I do not
sleep well here. I suppose the air being so strong, one has to get used to it;
also I cannot get used to the noise of the sea. Badge lies awake a long time too,
and asks what he is to do not to hear it. Fortunately Baby does not notice it and
sleeps well.   ..... Still, we get them out between whiles, and keep either near
the station or the house so as not to get caught. I have a bathe every morning and
the children a salt warm bath at night. ..... I hear there is a boat from Glasgow
to Coleraine, which goes on to Portrush. ..... You will be surprised to hear
that I went to church yesterday. Nice little church, next to no people, and the
clergyman played the organ also; there is a nice peal of bells which Mr Badge is
much interested in. .....

                                        Always your own
                                        Doli

Castlerock
17 June 1901

My own deal Lal

..... I can see you wrote in very low spirits, and feel that
I am to blame for having arranged our holiday in this way, I
had the idea that the children ought to get away as soon as
possible and so selfishly did not consider you as much as I
should; we should have come for July and Aug. Instead of June
..... There are only two or three walks about here, so I go
the same one nearly every evening; there is a walk round by
the cliffs that is nice, where I do not let the children go
at all for fear of accidents ..... . Here is a little story
of Babbins to amuse the old people. I took him to a shop to
buy and ld. Engine and the woman asked him if she should tie
a string to it for him. Baby just looked at her with great
contempt and said, "Baby doesn't see any string on the engines
what baby sees in the station". You never saw a woman so
taken aback as she was. Baby is just infatuated with the
trains; no matter where he is, if he sees a "siglan" down he
has to be taken back to the station. The porter took Badge up
into the signal box the other day, which has been his ambition
ever since he came down. .....

With lots of love .....

Doli

Previous photo: Christ Church, Church of Ireland, Castlerock

```
                              Clifton Terrace
                              Castlerock
                              22 August 1904


Jack's foot looks to me to be more swelled that it was, but
he does not complain about it hurting him and of course he
runs about the whole time which can't be good for it.   We are
thinking of going to Derry to see walls and the old cannons.


                              Doli
```

Towards the end of that summer holiday we have in Flora's letters one of the early references to the building of the new family home, Little Lea, in Belfast. This was probably the reason why Albert did not go up to Castlerock that summer, although from the records it is evident that Albert did not enjoy the annual ritual of a summer holiday and preferred to remain at home and at work. Flora includes in her letter a mention of her anxiety to return to Belfast to see the progress on the new house and rather poignantly writes about her feelings of loneliness and longing to return to the company of Albert even though she had not tired of Castlerock.

Castlerock marks its links with Lewis and his family in the 5m x 2m relief sculpture mounted on the wall of the Peter Thompson Memorial Hall in the village.

It was during these holidays that Lewis began his familiarity with the coastline of County Antrim and of County Londonderry. He came to know not just the two seaside resorts at which they stayed but also the surrounding area. In two of her letters written from Castlerock in 1904, Flora informs Albert that the boys have a determination to walk to Downhill, a village with a long sandy beach a few miles from Castlerock and of a planned visit to Derry which was a train journey away. These day trips and visits left an indelible imprint of the beauty of the shoreline, the vastness of the Atlantic ocean and the scenic landscapes.

Clifton Terrace
Castlerock
26 August 1904

My Dear old love

I am anxious to get up (back to Belfast) and see the house, I expect to see a
great difference. Poor Jacks has never been up since there was anything to see.
(this refers to the building of Little Lea, the new house on Circular Road in Belfast)

I am not exactly tired of Castlerock but I am lonely and shall be very glad to be
back with my dear BEAR in our own home next week. Martha will have a fire in the
nursery and blankets and sheets well-aired.

From your loving wife, Doli

Downhill beach showing Mussenden Temple and railway tunnel

Rock Ryan Cottage: thought locally to be the site for Bath Villa
which is adjacent to the site of 'The Baths'

Clifton Terrace
Castlerock

August 1904

.....   We had a comfortable journey yesterday, and the boys were very good .....
Jacksie and Warren are in one room ... and their window looks out on the railway.
They pulled up the blind and were settling themselves to a morning's fun but I got
them to go to sleep again. The boys have set their heart on walking to Downhill
this afternoon .....

                          Doli

Dunluce Castle

One of the prominent features of the stretch of coastline between Ballycastle
and Castlerock is the castle at Dunluce in Country Antrim which Lewis would
have seen as a child. The first views of it, caught from the winding coastal road
from Ballycastle to Castlerock, are very striking. It sits perched precariously
on the rocky edge of a cliff, high above the Atlantic Ocean. Dunluce Castle
has had a long and chequered history. Its early beginnings go back to the
fourteenth century when it is listed as a fortification in the Earldom of Ulster.
The castle was taken from the McQuillans by Sorley Boy McDonnell in 1565
and the McDonnells held it for over a hundred years. It is a well-known local
story that in a wild winter storm in 1639, the kitchens of the castle, which
occupies a commanding site high up on a hilly promontory, fell into the
Atlantic Ocean which crashes onto the beach below. After some restoration,
the castle was finally abandoned by the McDonnells in 1690 and has long been
a ruin which Lewis would have seen as a child. It is interesting that when
the children in his story of Prince Caspian return to Narnia, they spend their
first nights in the ruin of Cair Paravel, once a place of grandeur and awe as
described by Lewis in *The Lion, the Witch and the Wardrobe*:

Ruins of Dunluce Castle

Previous photo: Dunluce Castle and coastline looking towards Giant's Causeway

"Cair Paravel on its little hill towered above them; before them were the sands, with rocks and little pools of salt water, and seaweed and the smell of the sea and long miles of bluish-green water and waves breaking for ever and ever on the beach." (3)

Dunluce in the mist

This is a very fitting description of Dunluce Castle and its immediate setting. Just as time runs most peculiarly in Narnia, Lewis may have imagined Dunluce in its glory days as the setting for the coronation of the four children on the four thrones at Cair Paravel in *The Lion, the Witch and the Wardrobe*. By the time we get to *Prince Caspian*, the castle is a ruin and similar to the Dunluce Castle Lewis remembers in his childhood. The physical description alone may not be sufficient to merit the assertion that Cair Paravel reflects Lewis's childhood memory of Dunluce but a moment's consideration of what he does in the text of *The Chronicles of Narnia* gives to the assertion an interesting ring. The sentences immediately after the description of Cair Paravel almost at the end of *The Lion, the Witch and the Wardrobe* form a rather curious set of three short sentences, one ending with an exclamation mark and two of them with question marks. They don't quite make sense in the story and certainly could have been omitted without significant loss. They would, however, have been a great loss if his intention was to make an important if veiled link with the island of his birth. Unlike their immediate context, the questions seem to be directed, almost unnecessarily, at the reader. Having referred to the *sound* of the sea crashing on the shore and the wild calls of the gulls, he asks the readers in a very direct and almost personal way:

The walkway to Dunluce Castle

"Have <u>you</u> heard it? Can <u>you</u> remember?" (4)

These sentences are inviting an answer as to whether the reader can share this real memory, a memory that was for him drawn from his earliest childhood. Setting this alongside the ending of the final book in the *Chronicles* makes the suggestion even more interesting. In the penultimate chapter of *The Last Battle*, after the Narnians have ventured through the stable door and are commanded by Aslan himself that they should go further up and further in to the new place where they find themselves, a new memory is discussed. As they progressed in this new, fresh land, Lucy asked Peter where he supposed they were. Peter replied with a telling comment:

"'I don't know,' said the *High King* [an Irish idea in itself]. *'It reminds me of somewhere* [notice the appeal to memory] *but I can't give it a name. Could it be somewhere we once stayed for a <u>holiday</u> when we were very, very small? '* ... *'It would have to have been a jolly good holiday,'* said Eustace... *'I bet there isn't a country like this anywhere in our world. Is it not Aslan's Country?'* said Tirian." (5)

The narrative moves on with these questions about their location when suddenly Farsight the eagle swoops down from his lofty perspective and says:

"'Kings and Queens, we have all been blind. From up there I have seen it all ... the great river and Cair Paravel still shining on the <u>edge</u> of the eastern Sea. Narnia is not dead. This is Narnia... I have come Home *at last! This is my real country! I belong here, this is the land I have been looking for all my life ... come further up and further in'."* (6)

County Down

For all of his life Lewis retained a fondness for County Down that began in his childhood and before he was six years of age. His first aesthetic experiences and his first encounter with longing and with all that was good have associations with County Down. We have Lewis's own record as outlined in the opening chapter of *Surprised by Joy*, as the authority on which to base this assertion.

"As long as I live my imagination of Paradise will retain something of my brother's toy garden. And every day there were what we called the 'Green Hills'; that is, the low line of the Castlereagh Hills which we saw from the nursery windows. They

were not very far off but they were, to children, quite unattainable. They taught
me longing – Sehnsucht; made me for good or ill and before I was six years old, a
votary of the Blue Flower." (7)

These feelings that Lewis records were observed in and remembered from his
childhood, but triggered by the view of the County Down hillside seen in the
distance from the place of his birth.

In addition to these earliest memories of the County Down
landscape as seen from the windows of their house, Flora took
the boys to two County Down locations for their summer holidays
of 1903 and 1905. Both holidays are recorded in letters written
by Flora from their hotels to Albert. The 1903 letters are written
from the Spa Hotel, Ballynahinch, and in the letter of 11 May
1903 in that year there is a reference to the interest of both boys
in chess. Jack had requested a set of chess pieces from his father

Castlereagh Hills

and while they were waiting for the chess pieces to arrive by post, Warnie and
Flora improvised by drawing and cutting out of card a set of pieces. She taught
the boys the moves on a board they made from drawing blocks. The summer
of 1905 saw another excursion out into County Down for their holiday at the
Bangor Arms Hotel in Killough. The letters tell us of their visit to the lighthouse
at St John's Point which impressed the boys immensely, especially the sounding
of the foghorn which is still on the site today. The letters also record a day trip
with Flora's brother Gus and his wife Annie to Ardglass, a picturesque seaside
town close to Killough.

Photo below: View of Scrabo, Strangford Lough and County Down landscape

Scrabo Tower Newtownards

There is a lengthy passage in *SBJ* where Lewis describes some of the events of the period from 1914 – 1916. Strangely, while he refers to these years as the Bookham period, that is, the years he spent under the tuition of W.T. Kirkpatrick in Surrey, most of the description is of the holiday periods spent in Belfast with Warnie who was on leave from his duties in the army. It was during these months that his friendship with Arthur Greeves, whom Lewis first encountered at Campbell College, began to deepen and it was with Arthur that he shared his appreciation for:

"the country I grew up in" (8).

Although Lewis was smitten by the unattainable "green hills" seen through the nursery window ever since he first looked at them it was Arthur who drew his attention to the beauty of small details like:

"ordinary drills of cabbages and farmyards." (9)

He describes his main haunt of those days as being the Holywood Hills:

"...an area of County Down circumscribed by an irregular polygon whose lines run from Stormont to Comber, Comber to Newtownards, Newtownards to Scrabo, Scrabo to Craigantlet, Craigantlet to Holywood and Holywood back to Stormont..."(10)

Parliament Buildings, Stormont

He says of all of these County Down locations:

Comber town square

"...for the reader who knows those parts it will be enough to say that my main haunt was the Holywood Hills. How to suggest it to a foreigner I hardly know."(11)

Hopefully the images on these pages will convey the impression that Lewis would have wished to share with those

The Maypole at Holywood

of his readers of today who may not be familiar with the locale. He describes vividly the view of Belfast Lough as seen from the Holywood Hills and among the Lewis papers is a map showing the position of what he refers to as the 'Shepherd's Hut' or cottage from which could be seen his father's house and the whole suburb in which he grew up.

Lewis invites us to step a little way from this northerly and westerly prospect over a few fields and across a lane to behold the view looking south and slightly east. He calls it a "a very different world"(12):

Holywood shoreline

"...for here is the thing itself, utterly irresistible, the way to the world's end the land of longing the breaking and blessing of hearts. You are looking across what may be called, in a certain sense, the plain of Down and seeing beyond it the Mourne Mountains."(13)

During this period of his life he says:

"I was now happier than I had ever been, the holidays grew better and better." (14)

Some critics see a strong parallel between Lewis's actual description of the landscape as seen from the Holywood Hills with his descriptions of the Narnian landscape in, for example, *The Magician's Nephew.* In a reference to

Following photo: Mourne Mountains, County Down

Bangor Arms
13 Sept 1905

My Dear Al

I got the glasses all right and I find them great use. The house is very
comfortable and the food good. We went over to the lighthouse at St John's Point
yesterday; it was really too long a walk, but it did not look so far, and of
course the boys wanted to go. We went up and the man lit up for us, and showed
them everything and they enjoyed it very much. They make their own gas and work
the siren with a gas engine .....
 We are going to drive to Ardglass today, Gus will take Annie in the trailer, and
Lou will come on the car with us. The weather is good, I have not taken out my
umbrella since we came. The boys bathe every morning and are both well. Will you
come by the morning train on Saturday?

                                        Your loving Doli

The Old Inn Killough location of the Bangor Arms

Shoreline at Ardglass

County Down and the Mourne Mountains, Lewis says:

*"I have seen landscapes (notably in the Mourne Mountains) which, under a
particular light made me feel that at any moment a giant might raise his head over
the next ridge. Nature has within her that which compels us to invent giants: and
only giants will do."* (15)

```
                                        Bangor Arms Hotel
                                        Killough
                                        September 1905


My Dear Al

We got down very comfortably yesterday, but of course I found it hard enough to be
ready to start at 10:30.

This is quite a nice little place, it was beautifully fine when we got down, and
we had a nice afternoon; today is bright and fine too, but very breezy. The Hotel
is quite comfortable, very clean and the food is good and nicely cooked.  They
gave us soup, fish beef and apple tart for dinner an eggs and cake with our tea,
and milk and bread and butter at 8 o clock, so I think that was very fair for 30/-
(thirty shillings) a week

Ardglass is only three miles away, I think we shall drive round, they will take
you there on an outside car, stay and hour and return for 2/6  (two shillings and
sixpence) .  The man who drove the children and box up from the station, quite a
good little way, only asked 6d (sixpence) so car fare is cheap here

                                        Your loving Doli
```

Following photo: St John's Point Lighthouse, County Down

Oxford in County Down

Lewis's great love for County Down is perhaps best illustrated by a story
recorded by another Ulsterman, David Bleakley, who studied at Ruskin
College during the years when Lewis was at his zenith in Oxford. Bleakley
tells of his encounters with Lewis in Oxford and of Lewis's interest in David's
unlikely opportunity to leave work in the shipyards of Belfast and study in
Oxford. Bleakley met Lewis in a coffee shop in Oxford's Corn Market area
and Lewis on recognising the accent, introduced himself. They became
firm friends and one evening while walking together from Oxford out to
Headington, Lewis asked Bleakley to give him a definition of heaven. David
began an attempt at an answer using theologically loaded vocabulary only to
be interrupted by Lewis who said to him:

*"My friend you're far too complicated. Heaven is Oxford lifted and placed in the
middle of County Down."(16)*

Bleakley reflected many years later that as a definition it was not bad. If this
was how Lewis thought of County Down, it is little wonder that he returned
there many years later on his honeymoon visit with Joy Davidman after their
marriage in 1957. Details and images of this particular encounter with
County Down are included in the final chapter of this book.

The Mournes in a particular light

County Tyrone

Although Lewis makes almost no direct references to County Tyrone, events that took place there had a profound impact on his life and on his work. It was in Pomeroy, County Tyrone, in 1872, that Janie King Askins was born. Her father was the Minister in the Church of Ireland church there. Shortly after her birth, her father moved to take up the post of vicar at the Dunany

Church in County Louth and Dunleer where he was to remain until 1895. Janie Askins grew up in Dunleer and in August 1897 married Courtney Edward Moore who also was a son of the manse, his father being the Rector of Michaelstown in County Cork. Moore attended Trinity College in Dublin where he qualified as a Civil Engineer. Sadly his marriage to Janie was not a happy one and in 1907 she left him in Dublin and moved with her two children, Edward Francis Courtney Moore (Paddy), and Maureen Daisy Helen Moore to Bristol where her brother Robert was a doctor. Lewis met this family through almost a chance encounter which certainly altered the course of his life. He was billeted at Keble College, Oxford, prior to being sent to France during World War I with the Light Somerset Regiment in 1917. The dormitory accommodation at Keble was allocated alphabetically and Lewis found himself sharing with Paddy Moore. This and the Irish connection served as the basis for a friendship to form. Through this friendship, Lewis was introduced to Paddy's mother and sister and although, and partly because, Paddy was later killed in the ensuing

Pomeroy Village

conflict in France, the friendship between Lewis and the Moores continued and developed after the war was over. On Lewis's return to Oxford he shared a house with Maureen and her mother in Headington and eventually they set up a home, which included Warnie, in Oxford at the Kilns.

These arrangements had a profound impact on Lewis's relationship with his father who disapproved and who did not fully understand the relationship. Indeed, the 'Mrs Moore' episode had a profound affect on his life in general. Mrs Moore's temperament became increasingly difficult as her health deteriorated and life at the Kilns during this period had an element of drudgery about it that certainly became a restricting influence on Lewis.   Lewis does write in his diaries about this period of his life but records little of significance about his relationship with Mrs Moore.   Others have commented in differing degrees about this aspect of his life but since it was conducted in Oxford it is not the subject of this book.   Maureen married Leonard Blake and following the death in 1963 of a distant relative, Sir George Cospatrick Duff-Sutherland-Dunbar, on her father's side of the family, she became next in line to an estate in Caithness in Scotland and to a baronetcy. Lewis learned of this development just before he died and after Maureen's title was proved she became

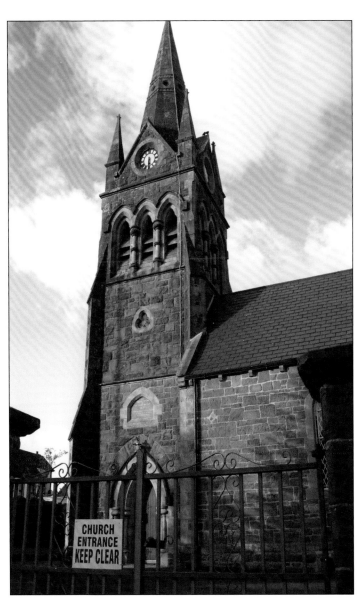

Pomeroy Parish Church

Lady Dunbar of Hempriggs in 1965.   This whole story of Lewis's meeting up with a family that had its beginnings in County Tyrone, the chance encounter with Paddy, the pact they made to look after the other's surviving family in the event that either one of them should be killed in the war, the years he shared with Maureen and her mother, the impact these friendships had on his life and the unimaginable twist in Maureen's personal inheritance are all fascinating and all arise from the link to the island of his birth.

County Donegal

Scattered here and there throughout his writing there are references to Lewis's visits to and appreciation of County Donegal. The earlier visits were undertaken and shared with Arthur Greeves and the later visits included both Arthur and Warnie. In 1916 Lewis returned to Belfast in August and he and Arthur spent part of their holiday in Donegal at Portsalon. In Chapter 12 of *Surprised by Joy* he describes the "Bookham days" as coming to a close and to the looming of his army service. He reflects on the summer holidays that had just passed:

Letterkenny bus station (formerly railway station)

"I remember, in particular, glorious hours of bathing in Donegal. It was surf bathing: not the formal affair with boards that you have now, but mere rough and tumble, in which the waves, the monstrous, emerald, deafening waves are always the winner, and it is at once a joke, a terror and a joy to look over your shoulder and see (too late) one breaker of sublime proportions that you would have avoided him had you known he was coming. But they gather themselves up, pre-eminent above their fellows, as suddenly and unpredictably as a revolution." (17)

Following this holiday, in his letters to Arthur dated mid- and late August 1916, he recalls the journey back to Belfast:

"The journey home was damnable; I had to wait an hour at Letterkenny and an hour and a quarter at Strabane. You may judge of my boredom... My father seemed in poor form when I got home and fussed a lot about my cold..." (18)

Later that month he comments in a letter to Arthur:

"Portsalon is like a dream. I heartily agree with you that it must have been nice to have the lounge all to yourself." (19)

Donegality

Donegal remained a favourite place to visit and he arranged several visits there in the late 1940s and early 50s in particular to Rathmullan, Co Donegal, which will form part of the next chapter. However, it is important to mention here a literary idea that Lewis came to call "Donegality". By the term -

'Donegality' he meant the tone or the character of a story, the feeling that it arouses and he felt that just as there are special places with a special aura so stories could convey a special feel or atmospheric quality.   This notion is used to good effect by Michael Ward in his excellent book *Planet Narnia* in which he deals with the special feeling that Lewis creates in each of his *Chronicles of Narnia*. He quotes a letter by Lewis in which he says:

Portsalon County Donegal

"Lovers of Romance go back and back to such stories in the same way that we go back to a fruit for its taste; to air for ...what? for itself; to a region for its whole atmosphere – to Donegal for its Donegality and London for its Londoness. It is notoriously difficult to put these tastes into words". (20)

These paragraphs and images attempt to provide some insight to and visual appreciation of the places first encountered in his early life and that impacted on C.S. Lewis. Hopefully some sense of the fondness that he retained for these locations in his native Ulster is captured in this sweep across the Counties of Ulster.

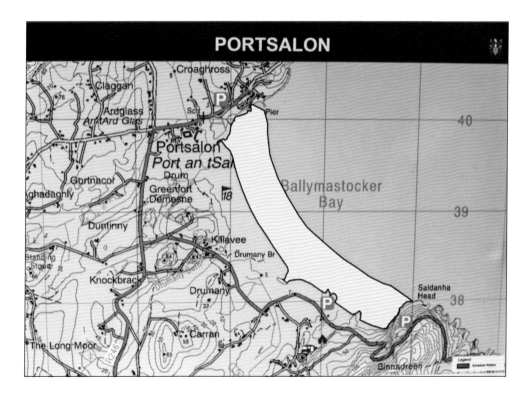

Entrance to Rathmullan House, County Donegal

C.S. Lewis in Magdalen

Chapter Four
—RELINQUISHING THE TIES—

SCHOLARSHIP TO OXFORD

There probably was never a specific point in his life when Lewis deliberately drew down the curtain on Ireland. He retained his fondness for the island of his birth right to the end and in the final weeks of his life there is a sense of regret that the old associations were inevitably coming to an end. At various points there were episodes, events, and visits that concluded significant chapters of his life and shifted the locus of his activity from Belfast to Oxford. His mother's death was undoubtedly one such watershed event in the life of the family as were the subsequent school arrangements made by his father. Although these events were significant in terms of determining the future direction of Lewis's life, they did not necessarily form a rubicon that could not have been re-crossed. Had the experience at Campbell College

been more prolonged it might have altered his route in life and perhaps resulted in a more permanent relationship with Belfast. However, as things unfolded, this was not to be. Equally, his gaining a scholarship to University College, Oxford, was a pivotal event. These years were formative in the friendships and associations he formed but it was the next stage that charted the direction he took, and established firmly his base in

Entrance to Campbell College

Campbell College driveway

Oxford for the second half of his life. His identity with Oxford is rightly and for all time secured in the minds of his readers of today. However, it would be a great pity if those who enjoy the literary legacy of Lewis were not provided with clear reminders of his beginnings in Belfast and the circumstances through which Oxford began to eclipse Belfast as the centre from which his work was undertaken. The Belfast element of his story is important because of his beginnings there and it is important to provide updated images of Belfast that enable enthusiasts to walk the routes so familiar to Lewis. It is also important to appreciate the circumstances that led to his gradual relinquishing of the ties to Belfast and the island of his birth.

Fellow

Without doubt his gaining of a fellowship at Magdalen College in 1925 was a significant event that shifted the focal point of his life to Oxford. The exchanges with his father in the years 1923 until 1925 indicate the concern shared by both at the possibility of his arriving at close on thirty years of age without a job or the prospect of one. Albert in 1923 had generously offered a further three years of financial support and the securing of a post at Magdalen after two of them, rendered the full offer redundant. There is an interesting communication over this event with his father in Belfast. First there is a letter to his father indicating that another job was on the horizon but little hope of securing it.

" ... A fellowship in English is announced at Magdalen and of course I am putting in for it, but without any serious hopes as I believe much senior people are in for it... These continued hopes deferred are trying, and I'm afraid trying for you too... (1)

On Tuesday, 19 May 1925, Lewis was informed that he had been elected Fellow at Magdalen and from that point at least the next five years were secured at Oxford and as his story unfolded, the direction for the next thirty years had been established by this event.

The communication with his father in Belfast takes the form of an immediate telegram to Little Lea followed up by a more lengthy letter some days later. The final stage of the delivery of the telegram to Belfast was by telephone and the scene is worth lingering on. Albert was at home and waiting for dinner to be served when the telephone rang. It was picked up by one of the servants, Mary, who announced to Albert that:

Little Lea

Little Lea bedroom windows

"...the post office is on the line". (2)

On going to the telephone, the message from the telegram was read to him by the operator. It was short and to the point:

"Elected Fellow Magdalen.   Jack."(3)

Albert's diaries record the flood of emotion that overwhelmed him on receipt of the message. He went straight to the bedroom used by Jack when he was staying at Little Lea and kneeling there, he gave thanks for prayers answered and for the fact that Jack's future had advanced from being uncertain to being in the category of a good start.

The letter dated 26 May 1925 to Little Lea that followed the telegram is a deeply emotional and thankful piece from Jack to Albert.   Warnie is very fair and precise in discussing the relationship between his brother and their father and indicates that while there was estrangement, there was no outward indication of the rift. This letter which comes chronologically at about the mid-point of the years of difficulty in their relationship is a warm acknowledgement of the unequivocal support provided by Albert and of the reciprocated appreciation of it. The letter is perhaps a high point, almost a touching of spirits in a relationship that was under strain. The letter contains several important sentences:

Albert Lewis and son Jack

*"First, let me thank you from the bottom of my heart for the generous support,
extended over six years, which alone has enabled me to hang on till this. In the long
course I have seen men at least my equals in ability and qualifications, fall out for
lack of it, 'how long can I afford to wait' was everybody's question; and few of them
had at their back those who were both able and willing to keep them in the field so
long. You have waited, not only without complaint but full of encouragement, while
chance after chance slipped away and when the goal receded farthest from sight.
Thank you again and again. It has been a nerve racking business, and I have hardly
yet had time to taste my good fortune with a deliberate home-felt relish..." (4)*

Although the letter contains the interesting phrase 'home-felt relish' the
episode was one that would weaken the link with home. The ties with Belfast
were being relinquished and the letters over the next years indicate that both
the relish and the enjoyment of
visits to home were on the wane.
His father's health from that period
on began a slow decline.

The Black Tie

While his father was alive, Belfast
in some sense remained in his
mind as 'home' and Albert's passing
was undoubtedly another of the
events that created a seismic shift
in the locus of Lewis's life. Albert

College Park East

died on 25 September 1929. Lewis had observed a change in his father
during his visit in September 1927. He thought his father looked older and
was acting more strangely but there were no other reported developments
until in July 1929 he heard from Dr Joseph Lewis, one of his cousins in Belfast,
that Albert was losing weight and in pain. Joe Lewis was a bacteriologist in
the Belfast Infirmary and had arranged for Albert to go into care in a private
nursing home in Belfast, Miss Bradshaw's in College Park East.

Albert was diagnosed as having cancer and Jack, who had returned to Belfast,
was informed that although his condition was serious he might last for weeks.
During early September Jack visited his father in Miss Bradshaw's Nursing
Home over a difficult ten-day period and later in letters to Arthur he provides

Site of Miss Wallace's Nursing Home, 7 Upr. Crescent, Belfast

some details of his feelings and of the difficulty of those visits. He left Belfast on Saturday 22 September 1929 to return to Oxford for the beginning of the new term but the following Tuesday morning received a telegram informing him that Albert's condition had deteriorated. Lewis left Oxford immediately to return to Belfast and arrived there on the morning of Wednesday 26 September to learn that Albert had died the previous afternoon. Although Lewis mentions Miss Bradshaw's Nursing Home where at one point in his illness Albert was a patient, the record of his burial indicates that he died in Miss Wallace's Nursing Home in 7 Upper Crescent.

Warnie at that time was on military duty in China and unable to return to Belfast in time for his father's funeral which was arranged by Jack. Jack's letters to Warnie provide a full account of the details including a story which contains a hint of dark humour that Jack thought both Warnie and Albert would have appreciated. Jack had travelled to Belfast in some haste on hearing of his father's deteriorating condition and on arrival learned of his passing. He had understandably travelled to Belfast without bringing a black tie. The wearing of a black tie to a funeral would have been considered in Belfast at that time to be not only appropriate but an essential mark of respect especially for the chief mourner. Lewis promptly visited one of Belfast's most upmarket department stores of the time to purchase the essential accessory. On completion of the purchase Lewis instructed the shop assistant to charge the item to his father's account and at almost the same instant he realised what he had done. He had followed the instinct of a lifetime in charging personal items in Belfast to his father's account, even on a day when, technically, his father no longer had

Following photo: The Robinson & Cleaver Building, Belfast

an account with Robinson & Cleaver. Lewis thought that both Warnie and Albert would have shared a moment of wry humour over the episode and so he records it in detail in his communication with Warnie.

83 Royal Avenue, Belfast

His father's passing marked a significant break with Belfast, even if the next eighteen months would mean numerous visits for the purpose of clearing and selling the family home. Lewis was accompanied by Mrs Moore on a visit to Belfast in December 1929. They stayed at Bernagh with the Greeves and used the visit to clear family items from Little Lea. Warnie did not arrive back in England until April 1930 and he stayed until December 1931. On 22 April, the brothers travelled together on the overnight ferry to Belfast from Liverpool and walked from Donegall Quay to Albert's former offices of Lewis and Condlin at 83 Royal Avenue. After discussions relating to their late father's estate and financial matters, Warnie and Jack took a taxi to the City Cemetery where Albert and Flora are buried. The next day, after some work at Little Lea and a visit to their uncle Gussy, Flora's brother, in Holywood, County Down, Jack and Warnie returned to Oxford on the evening ferry to Liverpool. The relationship with Belfast had changed. In the months that followed, the proceeds of the sale of the family home and the Belfast bank balances enabled the transactions that ended the relationship with Little Lea and commenced the association with the Kilns that would become Lewis's home for the second half of his life and would inextricably link the Lewis brothers to Oxford.

Regression

From the time of Lewis's appointment at Magdalen until his father's death in 1929, new friendships had been formed, old ones deepened and over this period other changes had also been taking place. His circle of friends in these years included Tolkien, Coghill, Dyson, Williams and others who at various times would become part of the Inklings of Oxford. With these friends came new ideas, new world views, new challenges and importantly, a challenge to Lewis's own atheistic world view.   Lewis had long since left behind any of the beliefs he had first been introduced to at St Mark's in Belfast.   His confirmation there as a teenager, undertaken to please his

Following photo: Interior of St Mark's church, Belfast

father, he describes as a confirmation:

"in total disbelief" (5).

During his return visits to Belfast in the years just before and after his father's death, his philosophical view had been changing and on

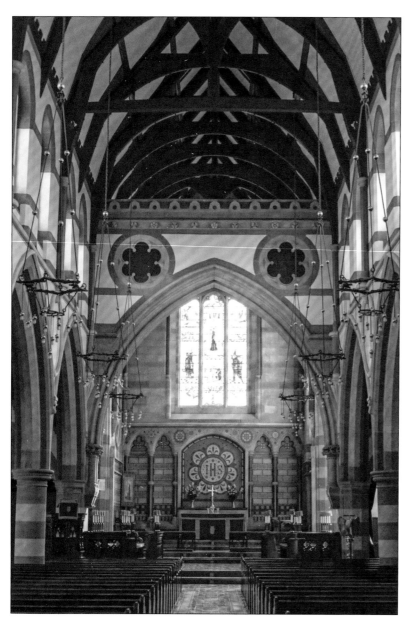

View along the nave of
St Mark's Church

the journeys he reflected on his intellectual journey in life. On 15 August 1932 Lewis boarded the overnight ferry from Liverpool to Belfast. His change in viewpoint had moved almost full circle. He had discussed with friends, debated with his colleagues and finally changed his view of myth and of historic Christianity. On the ferry he formulated a way of describing the change of view. He thought of this change in direction as a regression, back to something he had left in earlier years. His return could now be depicted in the form of a story of pilgrimage. On arriving in Belfast, since the family home had been dismantled, he stayed with his friend Arthur Greeves at Bernagh, the house just across Circular Road from Little Lea. In the two weeks that he stayed there, Lewis wrote *The Pilgrim's Regress*, his first serious book that slowly became a publishing success and put him on the map as a published author. The book was published in May 1933 and Lewis dedicated the book to his Belfast friend Arthur Greeves. There is a lengthy letter in *They Stand Together* dated 4 December 1932 in which Lewis acknowledges Arthur's editorial suggestions on the initial draft of the book and Lewis invites Arthur to comment on other aspects of the draft such as taste, jokes and contradictions. In light of Arthur's input to the book, Lewis

thought it appropriate to dedicate the book to him and to include a short
note to that effect on the flyleaf and so he writes to seek Arthur's approval
for the inclusion of the dedication and says of the book:

*"It is yours by every right, – written in your house, read to you as written, and
celebrating (at least in the most important parts) an experience that I have more
in common with you than anyone else."*(6)

The publication of this book was the first of many. In the other books, while
there may be hints of the beginnings in Belfast, the sharing of those early
drafts would be largely with the Inklings of Oxford. In contrast, the draft
of *The Pilgrim's Regress* was shared with Arthur. This book also marked a
change in the locus of the road before
him. Warnie retired from the army at
this point and settled into civilian life
at the Kilns in Oxford with Jack and
the Moores. He commenced working
on the many papers, letters and diaries
that had been brought back from Little
Lea to Oxford. These would, in time,
become known as *The Lewis Papers.*

Bernagh: Home of Arthur Greeves

Memorial Window

Over the period of winding up their father's affairs in Belfast and selling
Little Lea, Warnie and Jack had agreed that they would commission and
install a stained glass window in St Mark's Dundela to the memory of their
parents Albert and Flora. The commission was eventually given to a Dublin-
based artist, Michael Healy, then working with a group of artisans operating
under the name of the Tower of Glass. The window was completed and
installed in 1933.

It has a number of interesting features. As the photograph shows, the
window is in three panels, a feature about which there was little artistic
flexibility since all the windows in the church along the north and south-
facing walls are of this repeating pattern. Each of the individual panels in
the Lewis window is in three sections. In the top part of each panel there
is an image of a building, the central portion of each panel is dominated

Window in St Mark's in memory of Flora and Albert Lewis

by the portrayal of a male figure and beneath the feet of the three male figures in each of the three panels there is a clutter of small details, mostly of small buildings characterised by pastel-coloured gable walls and mono-pitched roofs constructed from red roof tiles. There is no difficulty about the identity of the three male figures. Their names are written in the glass. They are, left to right, St Luke, St James and St Mark, an unusual trio. The relative positions of some of the icons in the window are also unusual. At the top of the central panel is an image of the church, St Mark's, Dundela, in which the window is installed. There is nothing particularly unusual about its positioning since it seems logical that an image of the church itself should occupy a central and topmost position. However, if the same rationale for the position of the church icon is applied to the male figures, one might expect the image of St Mark also to be beneath the icon of the church and in the centre. Something seems to be not quite as it ought. The selection of St James, on initial consideration, also does not seem a fitting subject for the window that also contains St Luke and St Mark. If St Matthew, for example had been included in place of St James, some rationale might have been found in having the images of the writers of the Synoptic Gospels but the inclusion of St James necessitates some other explanation.

The fact that James is positioned immediately beneath the icon of St Mark's Church is also puzzling since it might have been reasonable to expect St Mark to be beneath the image of the church. There is a third puzzle. The Latin inscription at the bottom of the central panel indicates that the window is in memory of Lewis's father and mother and it gives their names and dates. The question may be asked as to what has been specifically included in the window that serves as a memorial to either parent, other than the inscription itself?

Some answers have been suggested. The first is that Lewis's father was Albert *James* Lewis and the James image is therefore included to his father's memory. If this is the reason then it is perhaps also explicable in similar terms that the figure of St James is holding in his left hand a silver chalice. The communion silver used in St Mark's was gifted to the church by the Lewis family and it is the Lewis silver that is used on some occasions for communion services. In Lewis's own life there was an element of estrangement in the common and family communion between him and his father and the symbolism might be that of a restored communion and of a restored Christian communion, given that Lewis himself had by 1933 made a regression back to the Christian tradition in which he grew up. It is almost as if, in the window, Lewis wanted to place his father centre stage and holding the symbol of a restored communion. There is also the suggestion that St James is included as the patron saint of the pilgrim. As if to emphasise this there is an image of a ship above the left shoulder of St James. The ship not only reminds us of a voyage or a journey but also of life's pilgrimage and the patronage of St James who is still associated with the European pilgrimages to northern Spain and the veneration of his final resting place at Santiago de Compostela. It is interesting that one of Lewis's Narnian Chronicles is *The Voyage of the Dawn Treader*, a ship on a pilgrimage to the utter east with Reepicheep as the image of the ultimate pilgrim. This notion of pilgrimage in the window is emphasised further by the three icons in the royal blue glass beneath the feet of St James that depict three of the accessories of the pilgrim: the pilgrim's staff, the pilgrim's purse and the scalloped shell, the badge of the pilgrim. All of this seems to serve the theme of pilgrimage associated with his father's name and it is important to remember the date. The year was 1933, just months after the publication of Lewis's first successful book, *The Pilgrim's Regress*, written in Belfast and dedicated to one of Lewis's closest Belfast friends.

St Luke

St James

The inclusion of an image of St Mark in the window is not surprising since that is the name of the church. However, it is instructive to note that the church icon for St Mark, the Lion, is also closely associated with the the icon for Venice, the city that holds the final resting place for St Mark. It is interesting because in the window commissioned by Lewis, the artist has wrapped around the shoulders of St Mark the image of a winged lion. The doorknob of the rectory of this church also has the embossed image of the head of a lion and the church magazine is called *The Lion*. The church itself is known to previous generations as the Lion on the Hill. These images had formed an enduring place in Lewis's mind long before he wrote about some of them and it is little wonder that when he came to write the Narnian Chronicles that the lion should come bounding in, as he put it, and pull the whole story

St Mark

together. These images were in his mind before the links with Belfast began to weaken and they reappear in *The Lion, the Witch and the Wardrobe* written almost twenty years later.

Photo below: Inscription on the Lewis window, *To the greater glory of God and in memory of Flora and Albert Lewis*

The answer to the question as to what in the window serves as a specific reminder of his mother is perhaps contained in the image of St Luke that occupies the central portion of the left-hand panel of the window. St Luke was a physician.   Lewis, in describing the events of 1908 regarding his mother's illness and passing, says that the family lost her, lost her gradually, lost her to morphine, to the illness and to the medics. His concluding childhood memories of Flora were of her being attended to more and more by the doctors and nurses and less and less by the family. The image of Luke would have been a fitting icon of these memories. In the window, the winged ox is wrapped around the shoulders of St Luke as the lion is wrapped around the shoulders of St Mark in the right-hand panel with its notion of service to mankind. The remainder of the small

Detail of the pilgrim's purse, staff and shell

buildings that fill the periphery of the window do not convey the notion of local architecture. They are, perhaps, more of Spanish or Italian origin and if so, they serve as a fitting memorial to his mother who spent the years of her childhood in Italy and whose name was Florence.

In early August of 1933, Jack and Warnie took a short trip to Glasgow or more precisely to Helensburgh, to visit two of their uncles who had moved there from Belfast in 1883. After this visit they travelled by boat from Glasgow to Belfast for the specific purpose of enabling Warnie to see the

Communion silver donated to St Mark's church by the Lewis family 1908

newly installed window in St Mark's. In a detailed letter to Arthur dated 17 August 1933, Lewis describes their visit:

"We trammed [meaning that they took the tram] *to Campbell* [Campbell College] *and thence walked up the hills round the shepherd's hut.   The sight of all those woods and fields made me regret very much that I was not having an Irish holiday with you: and the new house (near Kelsie's new house) made me wonder how much more might be altered by next year. We walked down by the ordinary, poignantly familiar route, stopped to look at Leeborough* [Little Lea] *– how the trees are growing! – and then went down Circular Rd to St Mark's to see the window which W.* [Warnie] *had never seen. He was delighted with it ….. Then after a drink in the reformed pub at Gelston's Corner, we got back into town."* (7)

Although there would be further trips to Ireland this one was significant. Installing the window in St Mark's and the visit to see it had an air of something that would not be repeated. It was a further and notable tidemark in Lewis's relinquishing of the ties to Belfast.

Stormont Inn at Gelston's Corner

Difficult Times in Drogheda

The period following the installation of the window in St Mark's and the
visit to see it is characterised by a lengthy absence from Ireland and a
marked slowing in the exchanging of letters with Arthur. Although the
correspondence was maintained, it became a trickle. From the late 1930s
and particularly through, and just after the years of World War II, the
letters at some periods became annual events. Arrangements for visits were
discussed but they did not come to fruition. Although the letters

were few in number they contain a "hunger", to use Lewis's
own description, to know the details of what was happening,
particularly to the people in East Belfast who had formed such
an important part of the fabric of his early life. Lewis's life
had become filled with the move to the Kilns along with the
developing routine there that included the Moores and Warnie
but there are also many glimpses of his longing for news from
Belfast. Lewis mentions on a number of occasions his fear that the
changes would diminish his recognition of the old familiar places.
From 1945 onwards, the letters from Arthur begin to record the
losing of old friends. This commences with the death of Gussie,
his mother's brother, whom he greatly admired, particularly in
his early years in Belfast. This was soon followed by news of

The former home of Forrest Reid, Belfast

the demise of Forrest Reid, another Belfast writer enjoyed by Lewis and then
in 1947, the news was of the passing of Mrs McNeill. The removal of these

Mature trees at Little Lea   Following photo: Annagassan Harbour, County Louth

Annagassan village sign

pillars of the society in which he grew up symbolised the reduction, piece by piece, of the reasons for returning to Belfast. With the removal of each piece there was less to focus on and only the memories of the people remained along with the memory of the stories they were part of. These memories mostly contained a bitter-sweet warmness but events in Warnie's life were developing that would take the edge off the fond associations with Ireland. From the letters of around 1947 it is evident that Warnie's difficulty with alcoholism was not only more evident but causing particular difficulties and anxieties for Jack. In the summer of 1947, Warnie had arranged to holiday in Ireland and to visit a former army friend, Colonel Parkin, who was, as things turned out, unable to meet up with him and Warnie found himself alone in Dunany, County Louth. This is an interesting coincidence in terms of location since

Annagassan shoreline

Mrs Moore had spent some time in Dunany as a child and Warnie's visit was in part due to his wish to get away from the company of Mrs Moore for a time. Not far from Dunany is the small village of Annagassan where Warnie and Jack had spent previous holidays together in happier times. The result of Warnie's solo visit to County Louth was that he ended up in Our Lady of Lourdes Hospital in Drogheda, where the Medical Missionaries of Mary, who ran the hospital, took care of him following one of his many drinking binges. Jack had to travel to Drogheda in response to telegrams informing him of his brother's condition and over these difficult weeks he got to know Sister Mary

Our Lady of Lourdes Hospital, Drogheda

Martin, who founded the hospital and the religious order that served in it. While Lewis was in Drogheda he stayed in The White Horse Hotel on West Street. During this time he wrote an article for inclusion by Sr Mary in a book celebrating the founding of her Order. This essay, entitled 'Some Thoughts', was written in The White Horse Hotel at a time when some of his own private thoughts in respect of his life and Warnie's must have been dark enough. He later refers to receiving a letter from Arthur at this particular time and on recognising the handwriting, he describes it as a friend's hand in a dark place. Warnie was assisted through the difficult period in Drogheda by the medical advice given by Dr Costello who was to become his doctor for some time. During this period, Warnie found his way to St Peter's

The Westcourt Hotel, Drogheda

Church of Ireland church in Drogheda and was a regular visitor there when he stayed in Drogheda. The difficulties encountered there were painful and no doubt they blurred the delight which both Jack and Warnie had shared on earlier visits to Annagassan, Dunany and Drogheda. These were difficult years in the life of Jack Lewis. Warnie's illness along with the increasing ill-health of Mrs Moore imposed a heavy domestic burden on Jack until her death in 1951.

The Westcourt, formerly The White Horse Hotel, Drogheda

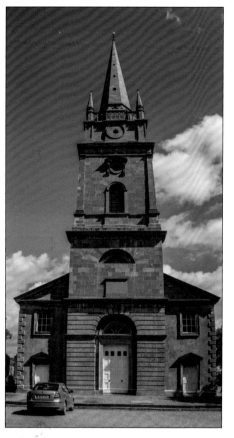

St Peter's, Drogheda

It was after this that Warnie's stability improved and saw him back in Oxford assisting with Jack's correspondence which in 1952 opened up the prospect of a new relationship which was to be the reason for renewed visits to Belfast.

The Old Inn

As already noted, the letters to Arthur are fewer in the years of the Second World War but after the war years there are many letters devoted to arranging holidays and visits to Ireland. One letter in June 1949 includes a wonderful ambivalence in his use of the word "home". Although the events described above undoubtedly marked a distinct shift in where Lewis lived and worked, he wrote to Arthur on Midsummer's Day, 1949. This was at a time when Oxford had been his home for many years, and he wrote to say that he was recovering from a short illness and had been ordered a complete change, presumably by his doctor. The letter is to inform Arthur of his intention to return for a visit to Belfast:

"I'm coming home (Belfast) for a month. I aim at crossing about 4 July – it depends on when I can get a sailing ticket. And of course I want to be with you as much as possible. Can you find me a nice little hotel (or decent rooms) near your cottage?" (8)

The nice little hotel that Arthur recommended was The Old Inn, Crawfordsburn, which was very close to a cottage, called Silver Hill, on the Ballymullan Road to which he had relocated on the death of his parents at Bernagh. Both Silver Hill and The Old Inn still remain much as they were when Lewis visited. This was to be the beginning of several visits to The Old Inn. The letters to Arthur are peppered with references to bookings of ferry tickets for the sea crossings to Ireland and accommodation at the Inn. One of these visits in July 1958 is of particular significance. After the death of

Mrs Moore, life at the Kilns took on a
more normal and predictable nature.
Lewis was focused on some of the
most important writing of his life and
Warnie was assisting with the daily
correspondence which was voluminous.
One letter of note, bearing a New York
postmark, was received from Mrs Joy
Gresham (née Davidman), that was to
initiate one of the final changes in the
Lewis household. The story of C.S.
Lewis and Joy Davidman is well told in
the film, *Shadowlands* and a number of
books have described the relationship
that developed between Jack and
Joy.   It was a part of Jack's life that
opened up a great happiness as well as
a great sorrow. Their friendship began
with the correspondence in 1952 and

Ballymullan Road towards The Old Inn

grew in spite of, or maybe partly because of, Joy's circumstances. Joy visited
at the Kilns and after their marriage, returned to live there, albeit with the

The Lewis Room at The Old Inn, Crawfordsburn

uncertainty in respect of her health. However, things took a turn for the better when Joy recovered sufficiently for Jack to arrange a short holiday and his thoughts turned to Ulster as the destination. He writes to Arthur in May 1958:

Silver Hill: 21 Ballymullan Road

"… And now, would you believe it? – Joy is so well that she and I are proposing to visit Ireland and should be in Crawfordsburn for 10 days in the first half of July…"(9)

In a later letter to a friend, Mrs Watt, Lewis described the visit:

"We had a holiday – you might call it a belated honeymoon – in Ireland and were lucky enough to get that perfect fortnight at the beginning of July. We visited Louth, Down and Donegal, and returned drunk with blue mountains, yellow beaches, dark fuchsia, breaking waves, braying donkeys, peat smell and the heather just coming to bloom. We flew to Ireland for tho' both of us would prefer ship to plane her bones and even mine could not risk a sudden lurch. It was the first flight either of us had experienced …We had clear weather over

Heather in bloom

the Irish Sea and the first Irish headland, brightly sunlit, stood out from the dark sea like a bit of enamel." (10)

The Rathmullan Hotel, County Donegal

In the letters to Arthur dated May 1959 there is reference to a further arrangement to visit Crawfordsburn and also Rathmullan in County Donegal. They stayed at The Old Inn Crawfordsburn and at the Royal Fort Hotel in Rathmullan. These letters and the visits to which they refer signal a further ending of the link to 'home'. Joy's condition deteriorated over the following spring and although they were able to take a short holiday to Greece in April 1960, she died in July of that summer. With her passing, another episode in the Lewis story came to a conclusion.

Previous photo: The Old Inn at Crawfordsburn

The Final Parting

Although the years from 1956 – 1960 had their fair share of difficulty they
were also prolific in terms of Lewis's work. He made the move to Cambridge
in 1955 and delivered his inaugural lecture there. He published a list of
books from 1955 on including, *The Last Battle*, the book that he considered
his best – *Till We Have Faces*, and *Reflections on the Psalms* among others. A
visit was planned to Ireland in July 1963. The intention was to stay at the
Glenmachan Tower Hotel in Belfast and then to move on to Castlerock,
the Glens of Antrim, Portballintrae and Portstewart. But this had all to be
cancelled because Jack took ill in July. His illness was so severe that in fact he
almost died. The cancellation of this holiday was indeed to be a terminal act
in relinquishing the ties with the island of his birth.

Lewis's study in the Kilns, Oxford with the vacant chair and the letters to Arthur placed on the desk

His final letter to Arthur at Crawfordsburn was written on 11 September 1963, just nine weeks before he died. It includes a number of significant references; he refers to the illness that prevented his visit to Ireland, to the fact that he had resigned his Chair at Cambridge and to Warnie, who was in poor shape in Ireland. His final words to his lifelong friend from Belfast were:

"...the only real snag is that it looks as if you and I shall never meet again in this life... I'm glad you are well ... but oh Arthur, never to see you again!..." (11)

C.S. Lewis died in Oxford on 22 November 1963, the same evening that was to see the passing of Aldous Huxley and the assassination of President John F. Kennedy in Dallas, Texas. The inscription placed on Lewis's gravestone by his brother was one that he first encountered in Belfast. It is a quotation from *King Lear* by William Shakespeare that was printed as a quotation on a calendar in his mother's bedroom on the day she died in Belfast in 1908. The inscription reads:

"Men must endure their going hence." (12)

THE END

APPENDIX

C.S. Lewis Tours of Northern Ireland

Through Belfast in the Footsteps of C.S. Lewis

To complete the entire C.S. Lewis Tour of Belfast comprehensively on foot would not be possible in a half-day. The tour route presented here is divided into two parts. Tour one takes in mainly the centre of Belfast and this could be undertaken in a morning or an afternoon at a leisurely pace on foot. The locations in East Belfast that have a Lewis association are presented as two options and each can be undertaken in about two and a half hours, however some parts of the walking tour option will need to be cut to make it manageable. For maximum enjoyment, the whole tour is best undertaken by coach and with a group led by an experienced guide with specialist expertise in the links with C.S. Lewis and his Belfast connections. For those travelling with a group or wishing to join a group it is recommended that enquiries are made through the C.S. Lewis Centre at Belmont Tower Tel 02890 652910 or at the Belfast Welcome Centre (www.visitbelfast.com)

Lewis Tour of Belfast City Centre

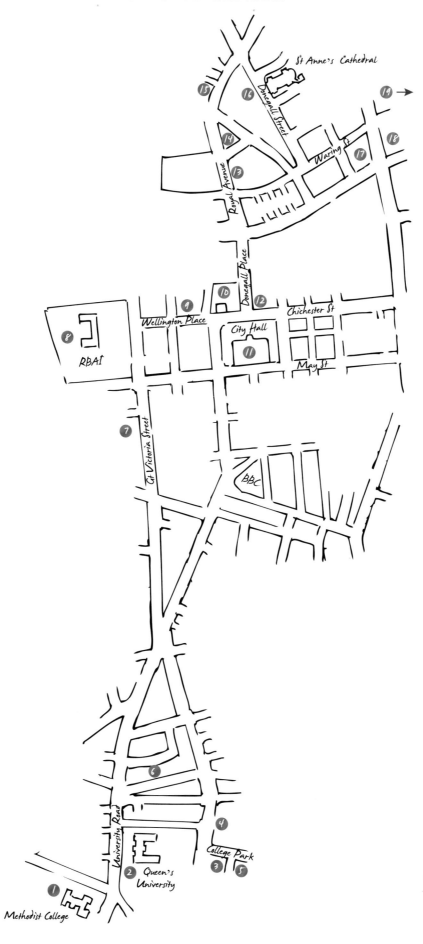

Belfast Tours

Tour 1:   Central Belfast
Walking from Methodist College to
Custom House Square. *Allow 2 ½ to 3 hours.*

The starting point for tour one is at Methodist
College.   This starting point is within a 30 minute
walk from the city centre but it is recommended that
if your starting point is City Hall, you should travel
to Methodist College by car, taxi or public transport
and then walk back into the city centre. Any of the
buses travelling south to either Malone or Stranmillis
will take you to the starting point.

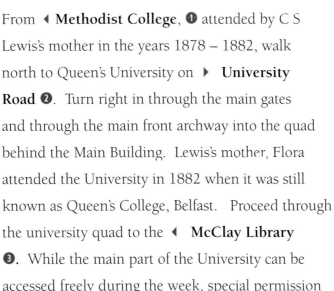

From ◀ **Methodist College**, ❶ attended by C S
Lewis's mother in the years 1878 – 1882, walk
north to Queen's University on ▶ **University
Road** ❷. Turn right in through the main gates
and through the main front archway into the quad
behind the Main Building. Lewis's mother, Flora
attended the University in 1882 when it was still
known as Queen's College, Belfast.   Proceed through
the university quad to the ◀ **McClay Library**
❸. While the main part of the University can be
accessed freely during the week, special permission
is needed to access the McClay Library which houses
the C.S. Lewis Reading Room and holds a series of
letters written by C.S. Lewis.

From the McClay library proceed along **College
Park Footpath** in the direction of the junction of
Botanic Avenue and College Park. Turn right into
College Park. Union Theological College ▶ ❹ will

be on your left.   W.T. Kirkpatrick attended Union to train for the Presbyterian Ministry. Proceed as far as **College Park East**. This terrace was the location of ❺ **Miss Bradshaw's Nursing Home** ▸ where

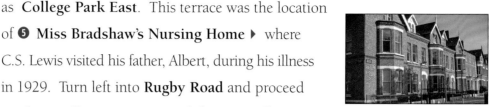

C.S. Lewis visited his father, Albert, during his illness in 1929. Turn left into **Rugby Road** and proceed north to College Green. Turn left into **College Green** and return along the other side of Union College to **Botanic Avenue**. Turn right on **Botanic Avenue** and walk on the left side of the street to the junction with **Lower Crescent**. Turn left into **Lower Crescent** and proceed west in the direction of **Crescent Gardens** and into ◂ **Upper Crescent**.

Number 7 Upper Crescent ❻ is on the left and is the location of Miss Wallace's Nursing Home where Lewis's father died in 1929. Proceed to **University Road** and turn left in the direction of the city centre through **Shaftesbury Square**. From Shaftesbury Square proceed north along **Gt Victoria Street** in the direction of the Victoria Street Station and the Europa Hotel. After the Europa you will see the ◂ **Grand Opera House** ❼ on the left.   Lewis refers in *SBJ* to family visits to the Opera House with his father and brother. Proceed along **Great Victoria Street** across **Howard Street** and with the Spires Conference Centre to the right you will see the ❽

Royal Belfast Academical Institution ▸ (RBAI) on the left. W.T. Kirkpatrick attended RBAI as a boy and also taught there before going to Lurgan College. From RBAI turn right into ◂ **Wellington Place** ❾ and continue in the direction of City Hall. On the left you will see a small shopfront at 11 Wellington place where Lewis first encountered the shop of T. Edens Osborne and where he first heard *The Ride*

of the Valkyries which Lewis refers to in *Surprised by Joy*. Proceed in the direction of **City Hall** and you will see the ❿ **Linen Hall Library** ▸ on the left. The library entrance is at street level but the library is upstairs. There is a coffee shop in the Linen Hall Library which is recommended as a good resting place on this part of the tour. The Linen Hall has a complete set of the works of C.S. Lewis and a few excellent first editions. It is also a good place to consult the reference books on the Hamilton family if you have time or inclination.

On leaving the Linen Hall Library by the front entrance, turn left on **Donegall Square North**. Just across the street is the ◂ **City Hall** ⓫. The construction of the City Hall commenced in 1898, the year of Lewis's birth in the city and at which time his father was solicitor to Belfast City Corporation. Opposite the City Hall is the ⓬ **Robinson & Cleaver Building** ▸ with its clock facing the City Hall. It was here that Lewis purchased the black tie to attend his father's funeral in 1929. From the Robinson & Cleaver building walk north along **Donegall Place** to **Royal Avenue**. At the junction of Rosemary Street to the right, you will see the ◂ **HSBC bank** ⓭. This was formerly the site of Royal Avenue Hotel which in 1894 was simply called the Avenue Hotel. It was here that Albert and Flora Lewis held their wedding reception after their marriage in St Mark's Church. Continue along Royal Avenue in the direction of North Street and you will see on the left a long terrace of red-brick buildings. The ground floor is currently a clothing retailer called Cult at ⓮ **83 Royal Avenue** ▸ . These were formerly the

offices of Lewis and Condlin, the legal practice of C.S. Lewis's father.

From 83 Royal Avenue continue north in the direction of **Donegall Street**. Note the offices of the ◀ *Belfast Telegraph* ❶❺ on the left. In 1929 the *Telegraph* carried a detailed obituary to mark the passing of Albert Lewis. After passing the *Belfast Telegraph* office turn right into Donegall Street. **St Anne's Cathedral** ▶ will be on the left. Directly opposite the Cathedral is a ❶❻ **Writers' Square**, ▶ a paved open area that commemorates twenty-seven of Belfast's most noted authors. Note the inscription on the memorial stone to C.S. Lewis and also the memorial stone to Belfast poet Louis MacNeice who was one of Lewis's students at Oxford. Note also in passing the inscription to Forrest Reid, another author from East Belfast known to Lewis and referenced in his letters.

On leaving the square opposite the Cathedral, which in itself is worth a visit, continue east to the end of Donegall Street and turn left into Waring Street. You will pass the ◀ **Merchant Hotel** ❶❼ on the right. All the rooms in the Merchant are named after Northern Ireland's most famous artists, poets and authors. It has a rooftop garden room from which there are excellent views over the city. Good for a break if the weather is fine. One of the top four suites in the hotel is the C.S. Lewis suite.

On leaving the Merchant Hotel at the Waring Street entrance, turn right and walk to the end of Waring Street. Note the view of the Cave Hill to the left. The profile of the hill as seen from this point is said to have been the inspiration for Jonathan Swift to write *Gulliver's Travels* one of Lewis's favourite books during his childhood (see *Surprised By Joy*)

Cross **Victoria Street** to the water feature to the right of the Albert Memorial, with its four-face clock at the top of the tower. Behind the Clock Tower is the Custom House. At the steps up to the entrance, note the plaque to Anthony Trollope referenced by Lewis in *SBJ*. The site of the ⓲ **Custom House** ▶  was formerly the site of the Harbour Board with whom C.S. Lewis's grandfather Richard Lewis worked on leaving the business he started with John H. MacIlwaine in 1868.

This point ends the C.S. Lewis Tour of central Belfast. There are two options from this point, depending on your transport arrangements.

Lewis Tour of East Belfast

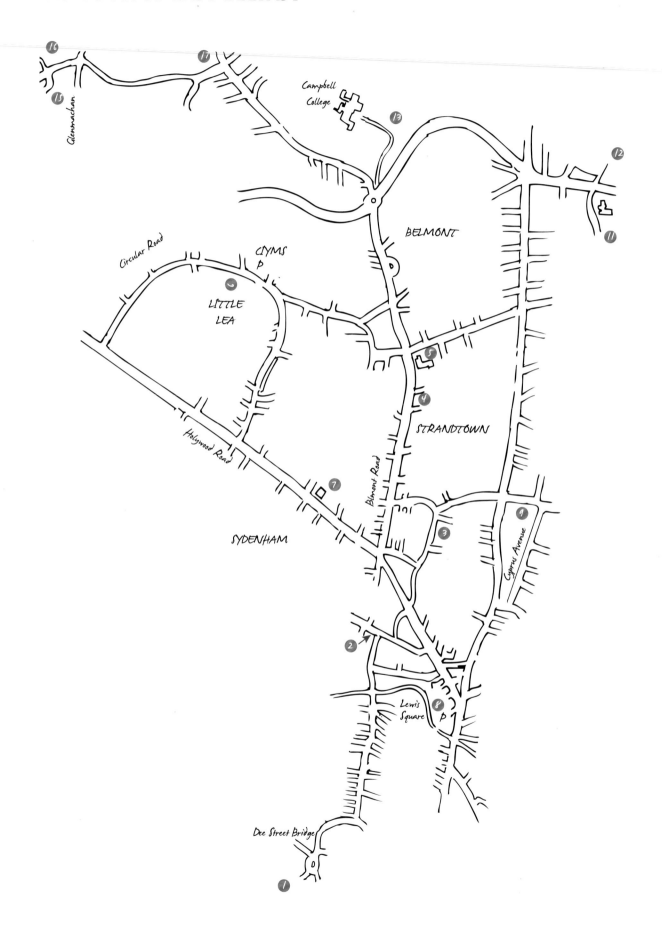

Tour 2:   East Belfast

Option 1 –
By coach or car and for those with plenty of time.
2 ½ - 3 hours

If travelling by car or taxi it is recommended that you proceed from the **Custom House** to East Belfast, crossing the River Lagan using Queen Elizabeth Bridge and following the route along Queen's Quay past the Odyssey/W5 building to the left. At the junction with Queen's Road and Sydenham Road, note the Belfast ❶ **HQ of CITI BANK** ▸ on the left (not shown on the map). This site was the location of MacIlwaine and Lewis, the shipbuilding business started by Richard Lewis, C.S. Lewis's grandfather.

Proceed east along Sydenham Road to **Dee Street Bridge**. Note the large yellow cranes of Harland & Wolff.   It was shipbuilding that brought the Lewis family to Belfast. Cross the bridge and immediately turn left into **Mersey Street**. This area before it was redeveloped was the location of the houses lived in by the shipyard workers when Harland & Wolff was at its peak. Continue along Mersey Street until it becomes Parkgate Avenue after crossing the Connswater River. Just before the end of Parkgate Avenue and on the left side is a row of red-brick semi-detached houses. Look carefully between the gaps of the houses and down a small laneway. You will see ◂ **Ty-isa**, ❷ the house bought by Richard Lewis for his family after they moved from Dublin and Mountpottinger. It was from here that Albert Lewis was sent to boarding school in Lurgan.

After leaving Ty-isa turn right on **Connsbrook Avenue** and continue until it meets the Holywood Road. Turn left and proceed to Dundela Avenue on the right. Drive up ❸ **Dundela Avenue** ▶ to a small parking bay on the left. Just opposite this, on the right is a block of brick apartment buildings with a blue plaque which marks the ▶ **birthplace of C.S. Lewis**. It was in the garden of the house formerly on this site that Lewis had his first experience of joy referenced in *Surprised by Joy*.

From Lewis's birthplace continue along Dundela Avenue until it joins the Belmont Road. Turn right and travel east in the direction away from the city centre. On the right you will pass ◀ **191 Belmont Road** ❹, the location of Lisnadene, the former home of the McNeill Family built in the same style as the existing Veterinary Hospital beside it. Proceed along the Belmont Road to ▶ **Belmont Tower** ❺, formerly the primary school. Belmont Tower has a small C.S. Lewis Exhibition in the Millar Room which is normally open. There is also a coffee shop in Belmont Tower which is the perfect place to stop for a break midway round the tour of East Belfast.

From Belmont Tower turn left and proceed along Belmont Church Road in the direction of Belmont Presbyterian Church. Turn right along **Sydenham Avenue** and continue until it joins Circular Road. Turn right at the junction and stop in the car park at CIYMS sports pavilion. Across the street is number 76 Circular Road, ◀ **Little Lea** ❻, the former home of the Lewis family. Note the plaque on the upper part of the house and to the front.

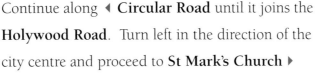

Continue along ◀ **Circular Road** until it joins the **Holywood Road**. Turn left in the direction of the city centre and proceed to **St Mark's Church** ▶ ❼, its tall tower and spire are visible clearly along the length of the Holywood Road. The church is not normally open unless arrangements are made through specialist guides. Note the church, ◀ **the old rectory** and **the Lewis window** which is best appreciated from inside the church. C.S. Lewis was baptised here in 1899 by his grandfather. His grandfather was the rector of St Mark's from 1878 until 1900. After leaving the church continue along the Holywood Road in the direction of the city centre to the library at **Holywood Arches** Health Centre. You may wish to use the busy car park which is accessed by turning right at **Westminster Street**. Beside the library is the ❽ **Searcher Sculpture**. ▶ The sculpture was erected in 1998 to mark the centenary of Lewis's birth. At the sculpture note the letter on the back of the wardrobe and the artist's note on the identity of the figure. Also note the designation in the pavement. The tour could be concluded at this point but enthusiasts wishing to explore further links with Lewis may wish to proceed to locations ❾ – ⓱. Some of these locations are identified only in references in the Lewis papers.

From 'The Searcher' proceed east, away from the centre of the city along the Newtownards Road to the junction with the Beersbridge Road. Turn right and you will come to Cyprus Avenue on the left. Proceed along Cyprus Avenue almost to the end at the junction with the North Road.

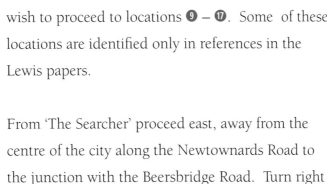

◀ **Sandycroft ❾** (no longer marked as such), the home of Albert Lewis's brother Joseph, is on the left. Sandycroft is identified as Joseph Lewis's residence on the inscription on his gravestone at Belfast City Cemetery. On leaving the location of Sandycroft turn left along North Road and note **Cyprus Gardens** ▶ on the right. The home of **Annie Harpur ❿** (Lewis's private tutor before he went to boarding school) is number 28 Cyprus Gardens on the left.

After leaving North Road, turn right along the Newtownards Road and proceed to the major junction with the Knock dual carriageway. Turn right and just past the Methodist Church on the right you will see Knock Presbyterian Church on the corner of the King's Road. This is a busy junction and the church car park is a convenient and safe place to turn. The site of **Knockburn ⓫**, the house that C.S. Lewis's grandfather retired to is adjacent to the church property.

On the other side of the King's Road is the site of what was **Canadian Villas ⓬**, the home of Gussy Lewis, Flora's brother. Gussy later moved from here to live in Ferndene, Holywood.

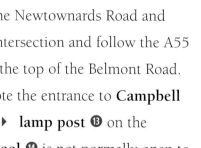

Retrace your journey back to the main junction of Knock Road and the Newtownards Road and continue across the intersection and follow the A55 to the roundabout at the top of the Belmont Road. At the roundabout note the entrance to **Campbell College** ▶ with the ▶ **lamp post ⓭** on the driveway. ◀ **The school ⓮** is not normally open to the public.

From the gates of Campbell College proceed up the Belmont Road in the direction away from the city centre past the traffic lights at the junction with the Old Holywood Road. Turn left at the **Glenmachan Road** and continue along the narrow and winding road until you reach ❶❺ **Glenmachan Park** ▶ on the left and ◀ **Glenmachan Retirement Home** ❶❻ at the Church of God site on the right. The Retirement Home was once the ◀ ▶ **Glenmachan Tower Hotel** ❶❻, an Italianate style house and similar to Glenmachan the home of the Ewart family referred to by Lewis in *Surprised by Joy* as 'Mountbracken'.

This is almost the end of the tour. For the interested enthusiast, the location of the **Shepherd's Hut** ▶ referred to in the Lewis papers and noted on a hand drawn map in the Lewis papers can be found by retracing your journey back along the Glenmachan Road to the junction with the Belmont Road. Turn left and drive countryward to a point where the Belmont Road divides into two parts, each called Belmont Road. Take the loop to the left and stop at the very top before it rejoins the main road. From this vantage point there is a clear view of the city and although no trace of the Shepherd's Hut remains, it was from here that Lewis could see his father's house (before the trees grew up). A short distance away from the top of Craigantlet Hill, there is the view over County Down described by Lewis in *SBJ* and from nearby there is a view of Scrabo Tower, the name he uses for a character in the unfinished Ulster novel.

Option 2 – Shorter walking tour of main locations in East Belfast. *Allow 2 ½ hours.*

From the city centre or if continuing the tour from Custom House Square, proceed by public transport to Connswater on the Newtownards Road at the junction with Holywood Road. Almost all of the buses stopping at Custom House Square will pass Connswater and the bus service is very frequent.

From Connswater commence the walk at the ◀ **'Searcher' Sculpture**, ❽ beside the library. Leave the library by walking to the rear of the Health Centre. Cross to the other side of the Connswater River and follow the path along the side of the river. The name of the river comes from Conn O'Neill, one of the Gaelic Chieftains who settled in eastern Ulster in the 1600s. Continue along the river until the path joins Parkgate Avenue. Turn right over the bridge and continue to the end of Parkgate Avenue until it almost meets Connsbrook Avenue. On the left you will see a laneway that is the entrance to ❷ **Ty-isa**. ▶ Turn right and walk for a short distance along Connsbrook Avenue. Turn left at a lane which is marked for the car park. Proceed up the lane to the main Holywood Road and cross at the top to Dundela Avenue. Walk along ◀ **Dundela Avenue to the flats** ❸ on the right. Note the plaque marking Lewis's birthplace.

From the flats walk along Dundela Avenue to the left until it joins the Belmont Road. Turn left in the direction of the city centre and walk past the Strandtown shops to the junction with the Holywood

Road.   Turn right and walk along the Holywood Road in a direction away from the city centre. Pass the Park Avenue hotel on the left and walk to ❼ **St Mark's Church** ▶ on the right. Note both the church and the old rectory.

On leaving St Mark's Church turn left, retracing your steps as far as Sydenham Avenue. Turn left at Sydenham Avenue and continue on after it joins Circular Road until you come to ◀ **Little Lea** ❻ at number 76 Circular Road.

From Little Lea cross the road back into the car park at CIYMS sports pavilion. Use the stile gate to access the path through Cairnburn park. Follow the path keeping to the right along the perimeter of the sports ground until the path brings you out to the A55 parkway roundabout. En route note the towers of ◀ **Campbell College** ⓮ rising from the trees in the distance on your left. At the end of the path the entrance to Campbell College can be seen on the opposite side of the roundabout. Keep to the right and walk along the Belmont Road back to ❺ **Belmont Tower** ▶ on the left. The tower is a good place to stop for a coffee and a break. There is a small C.S. Lewis exhibition in Belmont Tower and the bus leaves from directly outside to take you back to the city centre. The service is every 30 minutes so check the timetable at the bus stop on the way into Belmont Tower and time your leaving to connect with a bus to avoid a long wait.

Hope you enjoyed your walk.

LEWIS TOUR OF THE NORTH COAST

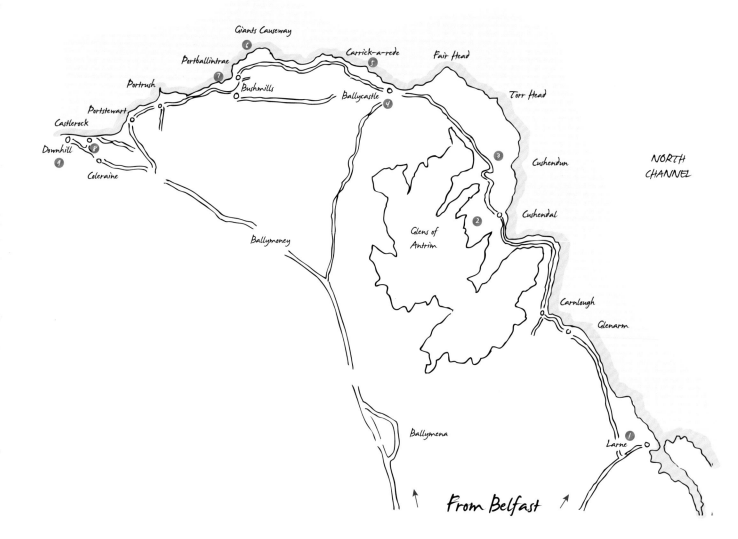

Giants Causeway

Portballintrae

Carrick-a-rede

Fair Head

Portrush

Bushmills

Torr Head

Ballycastle

Portstewart

Castlerock

Downhill

Coleraine

Cushendun

NORTH CHANNEL

Glens of Antrim

Cushendal

Ballymoney

Carnlough

Glenarm

Ballymena

Larne

From Belfast

The North Coast Tour

Tour 3:   Belfast to Castlerock
             and Downhill

This tour can only be undertaken by car or coach and
will take a full day to complete at a fairly leisurely pace.
If there is some flexibility in planning your itinerary, it
is recommended that this tour is scheduled for a day
when good weather has been forecast.

Leave Belfast by the M2 and M5 motorway heading
north and travel as far as Carrickfergus. Note the
castle on the right. It is worth a separate visit to tour
the castle and take photos but a coach stop here at the
beginning of this Lewis tour could leave insufficient
time at the end to complete visits to other points
of interest. Follow the signs to **Larne**. Note the
references to the Larne Road in Lewis's *Surprised by Joy*
where he records reading *Tamburlaine* while travelling
from Belfast to Larne. Continue along the scenic
Coast Road. If a bathroom stop is needed, **Glenarm**
provides a suitable parking space for a coach.
Proceed north to ◀ **Ballycastle** ❹ ▶ where a stop
is recommended. Note the hotel on the corner of
Quay Road and Main Street, the ice-cream shop and
the post box close to where Flora posted her holiday
letters to Albert. There is a pleasant coffee shop by
the harbour that will provide a pleasant break. Quay
Road, Ballycastle is the address where Flora, Jack and
Warnie stayed in 1901.

Leave Ballycastle and drive along the scenic north
coast to Carrick-a-rede. There is a good parking area

with facilities and the walk to and across the famous Carrick-a-rede rope bridge is an experience for a day when the weather is fine.   After Carrick-a-rede, the **Giant's Causeway** is a worthwhile visit.   This is a suitable stopping point for a light lunch. After the Causeway, note Portballintrae. This is mentioned by Lewis in several of his letters to Arthur Greeves as a place to book overnight accommodation for some of their walking holidays along the north coast.

After Portballintrae, ◀ **Dunluce Castle** is a must-see location for its association with Cair Paravel. Proceed along the coast road through Portrush and Portstewart. The Golf Club at Portstewart is a great place for a meal if a prior reservation has been made.   On leaving Portstewart drive into Coleraine and take the coastal route to **Castlerock** ❽. Park down by the beach and note the railway station, the C of I Church, Clifton Terrace on Main Street (Flora's letters of 1901 and 1905 were written from Castlerock and refer to these locations) and the mural on the Peter Thompson Hall which marks the village's link with Lewis by including the wardrobe with the other significant images associated with Castlerock. If time permits continue west from Castlerock as far as Downhill. There is an excellent beach at ❾ **Downhill** ▶ and from the beach the 'tunnel' referred to by Lewis can be seen where it passes beneath the Mussenden Temple.

Return to Coleraine and take the signs for the return journey to Belfast by the M2 Motorway which in normal driving conditions takes about 90 minutes.

Hope the day has not proved too exhausting.

County Down and the
Kingdom of Mourne

Tour 4:   Belfast to Bangor, Killyleagh,
             Newcastle & Kilkeel

This tour will take a full day by coach or car.

From **Belfast** ❶ take the Sydenham bypass (A2) in the direction of ◄ **Holywood** ❷, County Down. Holywood is a small town with attractive shops and always good for a coffee stop. Lewis and Warnie walked regularly from Little Lea by the back road to the Belfast Hotel (no longer there although the building remains) adjacent to the Maypole. From Holywood, proceed along the A2 in the direction of Bangor. On the left you will see signage for Crawfordsburn along the B20. In Crawfordsburn Village you will see the ❸ **Old Inn** ▶ on the left.

This is a must-visit location. Lewis stayed in the Inn when he visited Ireland in 1957 and 1958 when he brought Joy for a belated honeymoon visit after their marriage. Note also the Ballymullan Road. It is worth leaving the car at the Inn and walking to

number ◄ **21 Ballymullan Road**, the location of Silver Hill, the house where Arthur Greeves lived after his move from Bernagh in Belfast. A meal is recommended at the Old Inn at some point but a prolonged stop on the tour at this point will compromise the completion of the whole itinerary. Drive from Crawfordsburn into ❹ **Bangor** ▶ and stop at the car parks between the Abbey and the Civic Centre on the right. The Abbey is worth a guided tour. It is the burial location of Hugh Hamilton of Lisbane, direct ancestor of C.S. Lewis and

LEWIS TOUR OF COUNTY DOWN & KINGDOM OF MOURNE

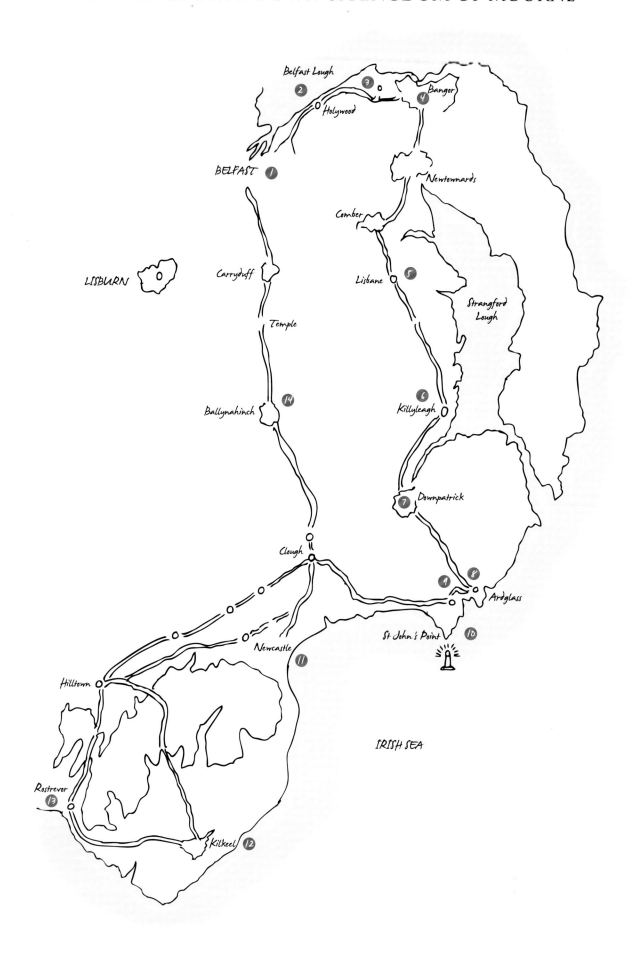

of Sir James Hamilton, a distant relative. The Civic Centre is worth a visit especially for those interested in the early monastic settlements in Ireland and Europe. The Civic Centre also has pleasant dining facilities which might be appreciated depending on your time of arrival. From Bangor, pick up the A21 road to Newtownards and proceed along the inner shore of Strangford Lough to Comber and on to

◄ **Lisbane ❺**. C.S. Lewis's ancestor was styled Hugh Hamilton of Lisbane. Today it is a small village with a picturesque little restaurant at the old post office.

Continue driving along the A22 in the direction of ❻ **Killyleagh**. ▶ This tidy little village is worth a stop. The castle remains in the private ownership of a distant relative of C.S. Lewis and it was to Killyleagh that Lewis's ancestors, the Hamiltons, first came from Scotland. There are two Hamilton burial plots in **St John's Church**. ▶ The tombstones that are immediately adjacent to the church wall are Lewis's ancestors. From Killyleagh continue on the A22 to Downpatrick. The St Patrick Centre is a useful

stopping point should lunch be required. There is a pleasant walk to St Patrick's grave in the grounds of the cathedral. From Downpatrick take the B1

Road to ◄ **Ardglass ❽** and then on to ❾ **Killough**. Today this is a small village but in the early 1900s it was a holiday destination mainly for people living in Belfast. In 1904 Flora Lewis took Jack and Warnie to spend the summer at the Bangor Arms in Killough and her letters to Albert were written here and record that summer holiday. The extension of the railway to Newcastle terminated the potential of Killough ▶ for further development as a holiday

resort. Flora's letters record a day trip from Killough

to Ardglass and also the walk to the lighthouse at

◄ **St John's Point** ❿. The lighthouse is accessed by driving from Killough in the direction of Minerstown and taking the road signed for the lighthouse to the left. The last bit of the path to the lighthouse has to be undertaken on foot. Flora's letters record the visit they made to St John's Point and also the delight of Jack and Warnie on being taken into the lighthouse and hearing the siren being sounded. After St John's Point drive through Minerstown and into Clough and here a decision is to be made. One option is to return to Belfast from Clough but if time permits there is a very scenic drive to **Newcastle** ⓫ then to **Kilkeel** ⓬ and along the B27 to Hilltown. From Hilltown the return trip can be made to Newcastle through Rostrevor and Kilkeel. There are references to all four of these towns in Lewis's letters to Arthur Greeves and they are also referred to by Warnie in his diaries. It was during walks that Lewis undertook with Warnie from Rostrevor to Newcastle ▶

through the mountains that gave rise to the famous qutotation, "*I have seen landscapes…*" which some commentators take to refer to part of the inspiration for Narnia. From Newcastle the return journey to Belfast will be via Clough and Ballynahinch. The Lewises spent a summer holiday in the Spa Hotel just outside Ballynahinch. Although the hotel is no longer there, Flora's letters recall the 1904 visit to Spa and Ballynahinch. From Ballynahinch, the return to Belfast is completed via Temple and Carryduff. It is now time for a short rest and then an evening meal at the Old Inn, if you are up for it.

Notes

Chapter 1

1. Lewis, *Surprised by Joy*, p 9
2. Ibid. p 17
3. Lewis, *Mere Christianity*. p 118
4. Lewis, *Surprised by Joy*, p 18
5. Ibid. p 17
6. Ibid. p 14
7. Ibid. p 14
8. Ibid. p 15
9. Ibid. p 20
10. Ibid. p 46
11. Ibid. p 65
12. Lewis, *Letters to Arthur*, p 452
13. Lewis, *Surprised by Joy*, p 20

Chapter 2

1. Lewis, *Miracles*, p 73
2. Lewis, *Surprised by Joy*, p 113
3. Lewis, *Mere Christianity*, p 152
4. Lewis, *Prince Caspian*, p 185

Chapter 3

1. Lewis, 'Dymer'
2. Lewis, *Surprised by Joy*, p 121
3. Lewis, *The Lion, the Witch and the Wardrobe*, p 164
4. Ibid. p 164
5. Lewis, *The Last Battle*, p 159
6. Ibid p 160 &162
7. Lewis, *Surprised by Joy*, p 12
8. Ibid. p 123
9. Ibid. p 127
10. Ibid. p 124
11. Ibid. p 124
12. Ibid. p 125
13. Ibid. p 126
14. Ibid. p 129
15. Lewis, *On Stories*, p 8
16. Bleakley, *C.S. Lewis at Home in Ireland*, p 53
17. Lewis, *Surprised by Joy*, p 147
18. Lewis, *They Stand Together*, p 128, 18 September 1916
19. Ibid. p 130, 27 September 1916
20. Lewis, Letter to Janet Spens, 8 Jan 1934

Chapter 4

1. Lewis, *Collected Letters*, 1925
2. Diary of Albert Lewis
3. Diary of Albert Lewis
4. Lewis, *Collected Letters*
5. Lewis, *Surprised by Joy*, p 130
6. Lewis, *They Stand Together*, p 452, 25 March 1933
7. Ibid. p 456, 17 August 1933
8. Ibid. p 512, 21 June 1949
9. Ibid. p 547, 30 May 1958
10. Letter to Mrs Watt
11. Lewis, *They Stand Together*, p 565, 11 September 1963
12. William. Shakespeare, *King Lear*

——— ACKNOWLEDGEMENTS ———

ACKNOWLEDGEMENT OF SOURCES

The author and publisher have made every effort to ensure that published or unpublished material used in this book by way of quotation or illustration has been duly acknowledged.

Permissions granted by copyright holders to use selected material are acknowledged below.

Quotations

Extracts from published material has been reprinted by permission as follows:

SURPRISED BY JOY by C.S. Lewis copyright © C.S. Lewis Pte. Ltd 1950
THEY STAND TOGETHER by C.S. Lewis copyright © C.S. Lewis Pte. Ltd 1979
MIRACLES by C.S. Lewis copyright © C.S. Lewis Pte Ltd 1947, 1960
THE LION, THE WITCH AND THE WARDROBE by C.S. Lewis copyright © C.S. Lewis Pte. Ltd 1950
THE LAST BATTLE by C.S. Lewis copyright © C.S. Lewis Pte. Ltd 1956

American Editions

Letters

Images

Photographic images used in this book have been provided from a number of sources including a substantial number from the author's own photographic gallery. In addition, the author commissioned photographic images and worked with Amy Gamble in adding to the gallery to complete the photographs produced in this book. The author has included a short tribute below by way of acknowledgement to Amy and her contribution.

Tourism Ireland, in addition to supporting this publication, also made available photographs from its gallery of images. A number of these have been included and their permission is acknowledged.

Belfast Visitor and Convention Bureau also made available to the author commissioned photographs from its gallery, a number of which have been used with permission kindly granted. 3 images: HICA0263 & (1)_CH_Antrim_0403 & A4510217
The photograph of the Linen Hall in Belfast is used by permission of the Linen Hall Library and the image of Donegall Quay was provided by the Ulster Museum.

Images of C.S. Lewis, including the part image on the front cover, are from the Arthur Strong collection. These images are copyright Arthur Strong © Ingrid Frazon and are reprinted by permission granted by Ingrid Frazon.

The Marion E. Wade Centre at Wheaton College also granted permission to use images of C.S. Lewis in their collection. Permission to use these images was kindly granted as is acknowledged.

Ordnance Survey NI (3 no. maps). This Intellectual Property is based upon Crown Copyright and is reproduced with the permission of Land & Property Services under Delegated Authority from the Controller of Her Majesty's Stationery Office, © Crown Copyright and database right 2013, permit no. 130032

Ulster Museum. Reproduced by kind permission of National Museums Northern Ireland. Black & White image, Donegall Quay.

Some images in the book were also provided by the designers and Martin Kenny is acknowledged as supplying images of Northern Ireland used in the book.

If there are any omissions in the identification and acknowledgement of sources, the publisher and the author will be happy to correct this in reprints or future editions.

Special thanks and acknowledgements

In respect of the sources used in this book and in the production of the book itself, the author wishes to include his personal thanks to a number of people whose technical assistance, cooperation and advice were invaluable in the course of drafting and compiling the book. These acknowledgements are included in no particular order but reflect the order of formal acknowledgements as listed above.

Rachael Churchill at the C.S. Lewis Company was one of the first people consulted at an early stage in the preparation of the draft text of the book. Rachael is an expert in her work and provided very precise advice which was of great assistance in the early stages.

Ron Hussey at Houghton Mifflin Harcourt assisted very efficiently in the final stages of preparing the book for distribution in the US.

Regular correspondence over a two-year period was sustained with Heidi Truty at the Marion E. Wade Centre in Wheaton Illinois. She has been great to work with and a source of not only guidance and necessary approvals but of encouragement in completing the task in hand. It is always an uplifting experience to work with a true enthusiast who is not just efficient at the job but who does it with such great relish.

The images included in this publication are the result of a team effort. The author wishes to record his appreciation to the group of people that he now regards as colleagues in the Belfast Visitor and Convention Bureau and in Tourism Ireland. They are too numerous to list individually but are represented by Gerry Lennon and Joe Hughes at BVCB and Aubrey Irwin at Tourism Ireland. John Killen at the Linen Hall Library readily agreed to search for and provide the image for the Linen Hall and Martin Kenny provided not only a major input into the design of the whole book but also provided images from his own collection to add to the other photographs. The whole design team are to be complemented for their input with special thanks recorded to Mark Thompson for his work on the cover design and to Cedric Wilson for coordinating the work and bringing the book to publication stage.

Amy Gamble.

In concluding this thanks to the entire cast of contributors, the author wishes to record a special thanks to Amy Gamble as noted above. Amy is a student at the University of Ulster. She is studying photography and in the summer months of 2012 gave several weeks to photographing many of the locations that appear on the pages of this book. Several expeditions were undertaken to Cork, Dublin, Donegal and remote locations in County Down in the pursuit of Lewis and his ancestors. She is a multi-talented student and readers of this book need not be surprised when they see Amy's work appearing prominently in the future. We wish her every success in her studies and in her professional career.